NEW Literacy Kit

YEAR 8

Geoff Barton

OXFORD
UNIVERSITY PRESS

OXFORD
UNIVERSITY PRESS

Great Clarendon Street, Oxford OX2 6DP

Oxford University Press is a department of the University of Oxford.
It furthers the University's objective of excellence in research, scholarship,
and education by publishing worldwide in

Oxford   New York

Auckland Cape Town Dar es Salaam Hong Kong Karachi
Kuala Lumpur Madrid Melbourne Mexico City Nairobi
New Delhi Shanghai Taipei Toronto

With offices in

Argentina Austria Brazil Chile Czech Republic France Greece
Guatemala Hungary Italy Japan Poland Portugal Singapore
South Korea Switzerland Thailand Turkey Ukraine Vietnam

Oxford is a registered trade mark of Oxford University Press
in the UK and in certain other countries

British Library Cataloguing in Publication Data

Data available

ISBN 978-0-19-832172-9

10 9 8 7 6 5 4 3 2

Printed in China by Printplus

ACKNOWLEDGEMENTS

We are grateful for permission to reprint the following copyright material:

BBC: extract from *BBC Science Shack* website 28.3.01, www.bbc.co.uk, reprinted by permission of the BBC.

Enid Blyton: extract from *Five on Finniston Farm* (Hodder & Stoughton, 1960), copyright © 1960 Enid Blyton Ltd, a Chorion company, reprinted by permission of Enid Blyton Ltd, a Chorion company.

Bill Bryson: extract from *Down Under* (Black Swan, a division of Transworld Publishers, 2000), copyright © Bill Bryson 2000, reprinted by permission of Transworld Publishers. All rights reserved.

Abigail and Philip Buckle: adapted extract from *Design & Technology: Graphic Products to GCSE* (OUP, 1997), reprinted by permission of Oxford University Press.

Kevin Crossley-Holland: extract from 'Arthur the King' in *Tales from the Old World* (Orion Children's Books, 2000), reprinted by permission of the publisher.

John Connolly: opening extracts of 'The Underbury Witches', 'Deep Dark Green', and 'The Erlking' from *Nocturnes* (Hodder & Stoughton, 2003), reprinted by permission of Hodder and Stoughton Ltd.

Roald Dahl: extract from 'The Umbrella Man' in *The Collected Short Stories of Roald Dahl* (Michael Joseph, 1991), reprinted by permission of David Higham Associates.

The Daily Star: 'It's sweets and sour...' opinion article, *The Daily Star*, 15.7.93, reprinted by permission of Express Newspapers.

Danny Danziger: interview with Des'ree: 'Best of Times/ Worst of Times', *The Sunday Times Magazine*, 11 March 2000, reprinted by permission of the author.

David Edgar: extract from Act 1, scene 1 of *The Life and Adventures of Nicholas Nickleby* (Michael Imison Playwrights, 1982), reprinted by permission of Methuen Publishing Ltd.

Emma Haughton: '50 Best...White Knuckle Rides', The Independent, 17 June 2000, copyright © The Independent 2000, reprinted by permission of *The Independent*.

R & W Heap (Publishing) Co Ltd: advertisement 'A Startling Memory Feat That You Can Do', copyright © R & W Heap (Publishing) Co Ltd, reproduced by permission.

James Herriot: extract from *It Shouldn't Happen to a Vet* (Michael Joseph, 1972), reprinted by permission of David Higham Associates.

Cassandra Hilland: 'It's For You', first published in *Times Educational Supplement* 5 May 2000, copyright © Cassandara Hilland 2000, reprinted by permission of the author.

Edna St Vincent Millay: 'What lips my lips have kissed' from *Collected Poems* (HarperCollins), copyright © 1923, 1951 by Edna St Vincent Millay and Norma Millay Ellis, reprinted by permission of Elizabeth Barnett, Literary Executor. All rights reserved.

Brian Patten: 'Simple Lyric' from *Love Poems* (George Allen & Unwin, 1981), copyright © Brian Patten 1981, reprinted by permission of the author c/o Rogers, Coleridge & White Ltd, 20 Powis Mews, London W11 1JN.

E Annie Proulx: extract from *The Shipping News* (Fourth Estate, 1993), copyright © E Annie Proulx 1993, reprinted by permission of HarperCollins Publishers Ltd.

Jamie Pyatt: 'Flying Solo', with graphics by Kathryn George and Stefan Bayley, *The Sun*, London, 10.11.00, copyright © Jamie Pyatt/ Kathryn George/Stefan Bayley/NI Syndication 2000, reprinted by permission of News International Syndication Ltd.

Henry Reed: 'Naming of Parts' from *Collected Poems* edited by Jon Stallworthy (OUP, 1991), reprinted by permission of Oxford University Press.

Martyn Symington: 'The complete guide to British Theme Parks' *The Independent*, 25 March 2000, copyright © The Independent 2000, reprinted by permission of The Independent.

We have tried to trace and contact all copyright holders before publication. If notified, the publishers will be pleased to rectify any errors or omissions at the earliest opportunity.

p13 Adams Picture Library; **p15** Austin Brown/Aviation Picture Library; **p18** James Davis/Alamy Images; **p21** Oxford Scientific Films; **p22** OUP; **p26** Universal Pictorial Press; **p29** Ardea; **p32** Camilla Marandi/Rex Features; **p36** OUP; **p44** Mary Evans Picture Library; **p47** Digital Vision/OUP; **p49** Hemera/OUP; **p51** Science Photo Library; **p52** OUP; **p59** Goodshoot/OUP; **p60** Alamy Royalty Free; **p62** Stockbyte/OUP; **p63** Michael Taylor/OUP; **p65** Stephen Frailey/Photonica; **p72** OUP; **p75** Robert Harding Picture Library; **p77** OUP; **p79** Stockbyte/OUP; **p80** Topham/Picturepoint; **p81** Hemera/OUP; **p82** Photodisc/OUP; **p85** Robert Adams/ACE Stock; **p86** Powerstock; **p89** Robert Harding Picture Library; **p92** Photographers Library; **p94** ACE Stock/Alamy Images; **p100** Photofusion Picture Library/Alamy Images; **p103t** OUP; **p103b** Cromwell Productions; **p112** Popperfoto; **p113** Popperfoto; **p116** OUP; **p118** Digital Vision/OUP; **p120l&r** OUP; **p122** Frank Lane Photo Agency; **p123** Frank Lane Photo Agency; **p124** Hemera/OUP; **p125** Popperfoto; **p128** Ronald Grant Archive; **p131** Hemera/OUP; **p132** OUP; **p134** OUP; **p136** OUP; **p138** Tim Bird/Alamy Images' **p139** Asperger/F1 online/Alamy Images; **p143tl** TH Foto/Alamy Images; **p143tr** Bettmann/Corbis; **p143b** Mary Evans Picture Library; **p146** Mary Evans Picture Library; **p148** Mary Evans Picture Library; **p149** Popperfoto/Alamy Images; **p151** Mary Evans Picture Library; **p156** Donald Cooper/Photostage; **p157** Donald Cooper/Photostage; **p158** Donald Cooper/Photostage;

Illustrations are by Peter Melnyczuk: **p155**; Oxford Design and Illustrators: **p39, 42**.

Cartoon Illustration is by David Semple.

Cover photograph: Mark Mason/OUP

Contents

Introduction

New Literacy Kit has been written to build your skills in English, develop your self-confidence, and make you an expert in working with a range of different texts. This new edition provides starters, texts, activities and assessment tasks which will help you to see what you are doing well and what you need to work on.

The Year 8 Students' Book combines texts from the three writing triplets:

◆ Inform, Explain, Describe

◆ Persuade and Analyse

◆ Imagine, Explore, Entertain.

These are based on the national curriculum for English (though we have linked persuade and analyse together to build your understanding of them). By grouping texts like this, you will be able to develop a deeper understanding of the way different text types work. This is essential preparation for helping you to write in a range of styles and across your different subjects at school.

As always in English, these categories will often overlap, but knowing that you are covering all parts of the English curriculum will help to build your confidence.

This is how each unit is organized:

Getting started

Each unit has a starter activity. Starters are great fun because they get your brain working. They lead you into a topic with lively, often unexpected tasks, which tend to involve minimum writing and maximum thinking. Use these activities to loosen your brain up, practise your teamwork, and feel your way into the main topic of the unit.

Learning objectives

The learning objectives help to map out the learning journey ahead of you. They don't tell you what you will do but what you will learn. That's really important – having a clear sense from the beginning of what you are expected to learn.

Introduction

This briefly sets the scene for each text, tuning you into the context of the material and helping you to know when it was written, by whom, and for what purpose. The more we know about texts in advance, the better prepared we are for discussing, understanding and exploring them. In this section, you may be asked to think about questions or ideas before reading the texts, or to make predictions about what might happen in them.

To do well in English, you need to have an understanding of why you are reading a text and how it relates to other texts you know. The introductions are designed to help you build this understanding.

Texts and activities

The texts have been carefully selected to interest and entertain you, and to help develop your knowledge of different text types. They are followed by questions, tasks and activities which are grouped in three ways:

- First, there are questions about understanding the text. These should build your confidence quickly by allowing you to spot key features and to show that you understand what the text is about.

- Next, you are asked questions about interpreting the text. These questions are more open-ended. They give you a chance to explore your own responses and to give your own opinion.

- Finally, there is a section on language and structure, which is a key part of your work in English. The work you do with language and structure will help you to become familiar with the language choices that writers make, and allow you to explore details at word, sentence and text level.

Writing activity

You can develop your understanding of the text further in the writing activity. It encourages you to see things from the point of view of the writer – testing out ideas, writing creatively and reflecting on your own language decisions.

Extended writing

Each unit gives you an opportunity to put into practice the skills you have learned earlier on. You'll be able to practise structuring your ideas, linking words and sentences, choosing the right vocabulary and making the right impact on your reader. The extended task always builds on the skills you have covered in the unit, so you should feel a real sense of making progress.

Assess your learning

This section helps you to review your own progress – not through formal tests and exams, but by helping you to evaluate your development against the learning objectives of the unit.

Speaking and listening

To make progress in English, speaking and listening is an essential lesson ingredient. In *New Literacy Kit*, listening and speaking are built in, from starter activities to assessment. In the process you should develop a better understanding of your own skills and qualities in speaking and as a listener.

Above all, *New Literacy Kit* has been designed as a lively and thought-provoking resource that helps you to make real progress in English. I hope you enjoy using it.

Geoff Barton

Getting started
Unit 1   Recounts to entertain

Newspaper reports often contain recounts. They retell events that have happened in a clear and often entertaining way.

1 Imagine a recount on the front page of a newspaper. It has the following ingredients:

- short paragraphs
- name of reporter
- name of newspaper
- photograph

- lead-in line (which acts like a sub-heading and summarizes the event)
- headline

- information about who, what, where and when
- caption.

With a partner, put these ingredients in order of most important to least important. Be prepared to justify your order to the class.

2 Newspaper headlines are rarely more than six words long. Choose one of the topics below and brainstorm three possible headlines to capture the readers' attention:

- a hot-air balloon had to make an emergency landing on your school field
- there was a major fire at a local chocolate factory – no one is hurt
- a strange wolf-like creature has been reported on some moors near Sheffield.

As a class, vote on which headline is most effective. What makes the winning headline so successful?

Unit 2 Autobiographical recounts

Autobiographical recounts tell us about events experienced by the writer.

1 Working with a partner, you have one minute to tell her or him about your best or worst memory. You might describe: a time you took part in an important event; a time you got lost; a time you were in an accident; a time you won something.
Try not to use 'and' or 'but' in your recount. Your partner must count the number of times you use these words. Try to use connectives such as these, instead: later; after that; earlier; beforehand; next; although.

2 Imagine you are writing your recount as an extract from your autobiography. With your partner, think of a first sentence that would grab a reader's attention.

Unit 3 Information texts

When writing information texts, it is important to remember the audience you are writing for. If the audience has specialist knowledge, you can use technical language. If not, you need to explain things very clearly.

1 Think of a topic you know a lot about, for example:
  - the options and shortcuts on a mobile phone
  - where to find and download free music from the Internet
  - writing and sending text messages.

Working with a partner:

a Give some information about one of these topics (or another of your choice), assuming your audience has similar knowledge to you.

b Give information about the same topic, but assume your audience does not have the specialist knowledge that you do.

2 How did the two versions differ?
  - Which words did you use in version (a) that you changed in version (b)?
  - Why did you change them?
  - Did you use any words in version (b) that were too specialist for a non-specialist audience?
  - Did you change your use of language in any other way (e.g. tone of voice, speed of delivery, use of gestures, length of sentences, types of connectives)?

Unit 4 Explanation texts

Explanation texts answer the question *why?* or *how?* The style in which they are written depends on the audience.

1 Imagine a three-year-old child asked you one of the following questions:
  - How do birds stay in the air?
  - What is money for?
  - Why do people have to go to work?
  - How is a sandwich/biscuit/cake/ toast made?

In pairs, plan how you would write the explanation. Jot down some notes, maybe as a spider diagram, considering: layout; diagrams; headings; type of words; type of sentences.

2 An important part of a teacher's job is to explain ideas so that students understand them. Without naming any teachers, think of three methods teachers use to explain things clearly.

Recounts: the essentials

Purpose and audience

Recounts tell us about events. They might include:

◆ autobiographies

◆ stories from history

◆ someone describing a crime he or she has just witnessed

◆ a newspaper story.

The audience may be familiar with the topic or writer, or it may all be new. It will usually be written in **chronological order** – that is, retelling the events in the sequence in which they happened.

Text level features

Most recounts will begin with an **opening paragraph** to set the scene, then give a description of events, and end with a **concluding paragraph**. Paragraphs will use **connectives** to link the sequence of ideas together.

Sentence level features

Recounts will usually use the **first person** (for stories and autobiography) or the **third person** (for factual reports). They are usually written in the **past tense**.

Often, there will be a variety of **sentence types** to create interest (e.g. several short sentences to build up suspense). Sometimes **dialogue** is used to move the story forward or to tell us more about a character.

Word level features

Recounts often aim to answer the questions: *who, where, when, what, why?* They may include descriptive writing, and techniques such as **simile** and **metaphor** to create more vivid images. They may use words that are simple or complex, formal or informal, depending on what the writer is aiming to achieve.

Newspaper recount
Flying Solo

Learning objectives

This extract is an informal, entertaining newspaper report. You will study the following objectives:

- Word level: recognize how a formal text needs appropriate word choice

- Sentence level: use complex sentences; understand the need for a variety of sentence structures; use a range of punctuation; adapt text types for different purposes; explore different levels of formality in texts

- Reading: make notes in different ways; follow themes and ideas; explore implied and explicit meanings

- Writing: think carefully about how a reader might react to your writing; present information clearly; explain complex ideas and information; describe something using formal language, where appropriate

- Speaking and listening: explain or commentate on actions or images; listen for a stated purpose

Introduction

Newspapers are written to inform and entertain. Occasionally they also aim to persuade – for example, in their editorial articles, which are intended to shape the readers' opinions on important issues.

Newspapers also use a range of styles. News stories may be punchy, dramatic, detailed, serious or sensationalist; features writing may be more leisurely, reflective, and personal.

Here is an example of traditional news reporting, from the Sun. Look at the way the text aims to communicate information quickly and to entertain us. When you have finished studying it, you will write a newspaper article of your own.

4.7.09   4.7.09

FLYING SOLO

Exclusive by Jamie Pyatt

Plane with no pilot takes off at 70mph and crashes mile away

A plane hurtled down a runway and took off without a pilot after he hopped out for a few seconds to make a last-minute check.

Glyn Hughes left the light aircraft with its propeller spinning and its brakes on to look for an airfield official.

While his back was turned the plane trundled forward, did a U-turn, then sped along the runway at 70mph and took off.

Glyn dashed back to find the £35,000 Grumman AA-5A had vanished and told the airfield manager: 'Someone's nicked my plane.'

As cops raced to the scene another aircraft took off and spotted the Grumman wrecked in woods a mile away. The bizarre solo flight was revealed in a Civil Aviation Authority report into the crash at Canterbury Airfield, Kent.

It told how London businessman Glyn, 48, hired the aircraft from a Biggin Hill flying club for an afternoon.

Glyn, a pilot of eight years' experience, was about to make

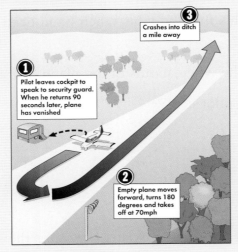

1 Pilot leaves cockpit to speak to security guard. When he returns 90 seconds later, plane has vanished

2 Empty plane moves forward, turns 180 degrees and takes off at 70mph

3 Crashes into ditch a mile away

his return flight when he realised his battery was drained because he had left it on. So he and a security guard used a car battery to start the engine.

As he sat in the plane waiting for his battery to recharge he realised he had forgotten to refit its cover.

So, fearing a roasting from the flying club instructors, he decided to get out and look for it.

He left the brakes on but kept the engine running fearing the plane would not restart.

The report stated: 'He believed the security guard had the battery cover so he ran over to his caravan across the airfield.

'He reasoned he could be back in 90 seconds.'

Character

'He found that the security guard did not know where the cover was. When he returned the aircraft had gone.'

The plane had moved forward, turned left through 180 degrees, gathered speed and then taken off before crashing into a ditch.

The report does not reveal how it started moving on its own.

Glyn, a married dad of one who runs his own electronics business, was unavailable for comment.

Instructor Dave Lawrence said: 'It's a miracle no one was hurt. The airport is near houses and a motorway.'

One pilot said: 'Glyn's a colourful character who's had his share of incidents – I wouldn't lend him my plane.'

A spokeswoman for the plane's owners Civil Air said: 'I think we would all have found it really funny … if it had been someone else's plane.'

UNDERSTANDING THE TEXT

1 Where did the incident take place?

2 Why had the pilot left the plane?

3 What were his first thoughts when he noticed the plane had disappeared?

4 How were the whereabouts of the plane discovered?

5 What is the pilot's:

- name
- age
- family
- job?

6 Now look at the way the writer organizes the story. Which of the following questions does the article answer first: Who? When? What (happened)? Why? Where? Which of these questions gets answered last?

Put the five 'W' questions in the order in which they are answered in the article. Number them 1 to 5.

INTERPRETING THE TEXT

7 Look at the diagram that accompanies the news story. Working in pairs, one person should use the diagram to explain to his or her partner exactly what happened with the aircraft. Make the explanation as clear as possible. The other person should listen and then say how clear the recount was. How could the speaker have structured the story more clearly?

8 Look at how much detail the picture adds to the story.

a Does the diagram contain all the essential pieces of information? Are there any other details you might have included?

b Do you think the diagram is important for fully understanding what happened? Explain why.

9 Throughout the story the writer refers to 'Glyn' (using his first name). Is this more or less formal than you might expect? What effect would it have had if the writer had referred to him as 'Hughes' or 'Mr Hughes'?

10 Towards the end of the article a pilot is quoted, talking about Glyn. Read what he says. What does he imply about Glyn and why the plane might have taken off without him?

LANGUAGE AND STRUCTURE

1 Look more closely at the headline. Even if this wasn't printed in large lettering, you would probably know that it is a newspaper headline. What features does it have which are typical of news headlines?

You might comment on:

◆ punctuation

◆ choice of vocabulary

◆ words that are left out.

2 News stories usually start with a topic sentence, which sets the tone of the story. Why do you think the writer uses the verb 'hurtled' in this topic sentence? Think of another verb he might have used.

3 Look at the fifth paragraph. Why do you think the writer says 'cops' rather than 'police'?

4 a What other examples are there of informal and vivid language?

b What do these examples of informal and vivid vocabulary tell you about the writer's view of his audience? What does he think they want from the newspaper?

5 Look more closely at the way the writer uses punctuation to help the reader understand his story. Use the questions on the next page to comment on some punctuation used in this text.

a In the first paragraph, why does the writer place a hyphen between 'last' and 'minute'? Would it make any difference if the hyphen were left out?

> # Hint
>
> - 'Minute' can be pronounced in two different ways to give different meanings.

b Look at the start of this sentence:

Glyn, a pilot of eight years' experience, was about to make his return flight …

Explain why the writer uses two commas around the phrase 'a pilot of eight years' experience'. Can you think of a different way he might have written the same ideas, using full stops rather than commas?

c Look at this sentence:

One pilot said: 'Glyn's a colourful character who's had his share of incidents — I wouldn't lend him my plane.'

Why do you think the writer has chosen to separate the ideas with a dash rather than a full stop? What effect does it have?

6 This activity helps you with note-making skills. Use a form like the one below to build up a picture of what happened to the mysterious aircraft. Fill it in using details from the *Sun* article.

Self-Flying Aircraft Factsheet

What do we know about what happened, where and when?

What _____

Where _____

When _____

What do we know about the person in control of the plane?

What questions are left unanswered?

WRITING ACTIVITY

The *Sun* article reports the story with a tone of fascination about what happened. In places, it has a jokey tone. But people living close to the airfield might take a more serious view.

Write a more formal newspaper report of the events. Imagine that your article is appearing in a local newspaper where readers will be seriously worried by what has happened, and concerned that nothing like it should happen again.

Your aim should be to inform readers about what has happened rather than to entertain them. Remember that this type of newspaper report uses the third person and the past tense, and aims to answer the questions: *who, where, when, what, why?*

a Think of a headline.

b Think of a topic sentence.

c Retell the story in 200 words, keeping the tone formal.

Think about:

◆ which information you will include (about the event, the plane, the pilot)

◆ how you will keep the tone of your story factual

◆ how you will show that this was a very dangerous event.

When you have finished, read through your work and think carefully about the effect it will have on the reader. Revise it if necessary, to make sure it gives clear information.

Personal recount
Going Surfing

Learning objectives

Using comic effects in a recount is an important way of entertaining the reader, as this extract shows. These are the objectives you will study:

- Word level: recognize how a formal text needs appropriate word choice; explore the meaning of words in quotation marks or used ironically

- Sentence level: explore a variety of sentence structures; adapt text types for different purposes; identify changes when a text is altered from informal to formal

- Reading: explore implied and explicit meanings; look at changes when texts are adapted into different forms or media

- Writing: experiment with language, implication and tone; present information clearly; describe something using formal language, where appropriate

Introduction

Bill Bryson is well known for his comic travel writing. He visits places and then describes the people, customs, and his own experiences there in a way that is designed to make us laugh. Sometimes the comedy is in the things that happen to him; at other times, it is the tone of voice he uses – mixing confusion, fear, dislike and a strong feeling of not being quite in control of a situation.

When you have studied this entertaining recount, you can practise writing one of your own.

The extract is from Bill Bryson's account of his visit to Australia, *Down Under*. His guides are an Australian journalist, Deirdre Macken, and a young photographer named Glenn Hunt. They offer to take him boogie boarding …

Glossary

evasively – *as if hiding the full truth*

abraded – *scraped*

unprepossessing – *unattractive*

Going Surfing

'What is boogie boarding exactly?'

'Oh, it's fun. You'll love it,' Deirdre said breezily but, I thought, just a touch evasively.

'Yes, but what is it?'

'It's an aquatic sport. It's heaps of fun. Isn't it heaps of fun, Glenn?'

'But what does it entail exactly?' I persisted.

'You take a kind of miniature surfboard and paddle out into the sea, where you catch a big wave and ride it back to shore. It's easy. You'll love it.'

'What about sharks?' I asked uneasily.

'Oh, there's hardly any sharks here. Glenn, how long has it been since someone was killed by a shark?'

'Oh, ages,' Glenn said, considering. 'Couple of months at least.'

'Couple of months?' I squeaked.

'At least. Sharks are way overrated as a danger,' Glenn added. 'Way overrated. It's the rips that'll most likely get yer.' He returned to taking pictures.

'Rips?'

'Underwater currents that run at an angle to the shore and sometimes carry people out to sea,' Deirdre explained. 'But don't worry. That won't happen to you.'

'Why?'

'Because we're here to look after you.' She smiled serenely, drained her cup and reminded us that we needed to keep moving.

Three hours later, our other activities completed, we stood on a remote-seeming strand at a place called Freshwater Beach, near Manly. …

Urged on by Deirdre, who seemed keen as anything to get into the briny drink, we began to strip down – slowly and deliberatively in my case, eagerly in hers – to the swimsuits she had instructed us to wear beneath our clothes.

'If you're caught in a rip,' Deirdre was saying, 'the trick is not to panic.'

I looked at her. 'You're telling me to drown calmly?'

'No, no. Just keep your wits. Don't try to swim against the current. Swim across it. And if you're still in trouble, just wave your arm like this' – she gave the kind of big, languorous wave that only an Australian could possibly consider an appropriate response to a death-at-sea situation – 'and wait for the lifeguard to come.'

'What if the lifeguard doesn't see me?'

'He'll see you.'

'But what if he doesn't?'

But Deirdre was already wading into the surf, a boogie board tucked under her arm. …

Let me just pause here for a moment to interpose two small stories. In 1935, not far from where we stood now, some fishermen captured a fourteen-foot beige shark and took it to a public aquarium at Coogee, where it was put on display. The shark swam around for a day or two in its new home, then abruptly, and to the certain surprise of the viewing public, regurgitated a human arm. When last seen the arm had been attached to a young man named Jimmy Smith, who had, I've no doubt, signalled his predicament with a big, languorous wave.

Now my second story. Three years later, on a clear, bright, calm

Sunday afternoon at Bondi Beach, also not far from where we now stood, from out of nowhere there came four freak waves, each up to twenty-five feet high. More than 200 people were carried out to sea in the undertow. Fortunately, fifty lifeguards were in attendance that day, and they managed to save all but six people. I am aware that we are talking about incidents that happened many years ago. I don't care. My point remains: the ocean is a treacherous place.

Sighing, I shuffled into the pale green and cream-flecked water. The bay was surprisingly shallow. We trudged perhaps 100 feet out and it was still only a little over our knees, though even here there was an extraordinarily powerful current – strong enough to pull you off your feet if you weren't real vigilant. Another fifty feet on, where the water rose over our waists, the waves were breaking. … I have almost no experience of the sea, and I found it frankly disconcerting to be wading into a

rollercoaster of water. Deirdre shrieked with pleasure.

Then she showed me how the boogie board works. It was promisingly simple in principle. As a wave passed, she would leap aboard and skim along on its crest for many yards. Then Glenn had a turn and went even further. There is no question that it looked like fun. It didn't look too hard either. I was tentatively eager to have a try.

I positioned myself for the first wave, then jumped aboard and sank like an anvil.

'How'd you do that?' asked Glenn in wonder.

'No idea.'

I repeated the exercise with the same result.

'Amazing,' he said.

There followed a half hour in which the two of them watched first with guarded amusement, then a kind of astonishment, and finally something not unlike pity,

as I repeatedly vanished beneath the waves and was scraped over an area of ocean floor roughly the size of Polk County, Iowa. After a variable but lengthy period, I would surface, gasping and confused, at a point anywhere from four feet to a mile and a quarter distant, and be immediately carried under again by a following wave. …

Perhaps it was the oxygen deprivation, but I was rather lost in my own little world when Deirdre grabbed my arm just before I was about to go under again and said in a husky tone: 'Look out! There's a bluey.'

Glenn took on an immediate expression of alarm. 'Where?'

'What's a bluey?' I asked, appalled to discover that there was some additional danger I hadn't been told about.

'A bluebottle,' she explained and pointed to a small jellyfish of the type (as I later learned from browsing through a fat book

titled, if I recall, *Things That Will Kill You Horridly in Australia: Volume 19*) known elsewhere as a Portuguese man-of-war. I squinted at it as it drifted past. It looked unprepossessing, like a blue condom with strings attached.

'Is it dangerous?' I asked.

Now before we hear Deirdre's response to me as I stood there, vulnerable and abraded, shivering, nearly naked and half drowned, let me just quote from her subsequent article in the Herald:

While the photographer shoots, Bryson and boogie board are dragged 40 metres down the beach in a rip. The shore rip runs south to north, unlike the rip further out which runs north to south. Bryson doesn't know this. He didn't read the warning sign on the beach. Nor does he know about the bluebottle being blown in his direction – now less than a metre away – a swollen stinger that could give him 20 minutes of agony and, if he's unlucky, an unsightly allergic reaction to carry on his torso for life.

'Dangerous? No,' Deirdre replied now as we stood gawping at the bluebottle. 'But don't brush against it.'

'Why not?'

'Might be a bit uncomfortable.' …

'Hey, there's another one,' said Glenn.

We watched another one drift by. Deirdre was scanning the water.

'Sometimes they come in waves,' she said. 'Might be an idea to get out of the water.'

I didn't need to be told twice.

UNDERSTANDING THE TEXT

1 How can you tell that Bill Bryson is nervous about boogie boarding?

2 What happens to him when he first tries to surf?

3 How can you tell from Glenn's reaction that 'bluebottles' are dangerous?

4 Why do you think Deirdre does not tell him the full truth about the 'bluebottle'?

INTERPRETING THE TEXT

5 As you read the text, you probably didn't expect that Bill Bryson would be able to surf successfully. How does his ironic tone help us guess in advance that his attempts will be unsuccessful?

Hint
● Look at sentences such as 'It was promisingly simple in principle'.

6 Which parts of the text did you find funniest, and why?

LANGUAGE AND STRUCTURE

1 a Look at the first section of the text. This sets the situation up for what happens later. Look at the range of sentence functions the writer uses. Try to find an example of:

♦ a statement

♦ a question

♦ an imperative (or command)

♦ a minor sentence (a sentence without a verb).

b In this early section, how does the use of questions make us want to read on?

2 The later sections use some complex sentences to explain the action. Find an example of a complex sentence that packs in a lot of detail.

3 Although recounts are often written in chronological order, Bill Bryson covers a number of time sequences in this extract. The first section describes him first hearing about boogie boarding. The next section moves forward in time three hours. Then he goes back in time for accounts of events in 1935 and 1938, before continuing with the description of his time at the beach.

a Find the connecting words which he uses to show the shifts to different times.

b How might he have introduced the flashback to 1935 in a different way?

c How does this use of different time sequences help to create humour?

4 Like many humorous writers, Bill Bryson uses similes and exaggeration, like this:

Simile

It looked unprepossessing, like a blue condom with strings attached

Exaggeration

I was scraped over an area of ocean floor roughly the size of Polk County, Iowa

He also uses some memorable phrasing, with metaphors like this:

… wading into a rollercoaster of water.

Each of these techniques adds to the comic effect. Find a sentence or phrase using one of these techniques, which you think is particularly effective. Write it down, and comment on why you think it adds humour to the text.

5 Look at the newspaper account Deirdre Macken writes. Her style is quite different from Bill Bryson's and also comic. How does she write differently from him? You might mention:

- ◆ the length of her sentences
- ◆ whether she uses the same range of sentences as Bill Bryson
- ◆ the way she describes Bryson's character
- ◆ the way she describes things he has not done
- ◆ whether her account is more formal or informal.

WRITING ACTIVITY

Based on reading this extract, what do you think are some of the secrets of successful comic writing?

Write an advice sheet for students, giving five tips on how to write humorous non-fiction (such as autobiography and travel writing).

You might mention:

- ◆ how to structure ideas so that it builds anticipation for later parts of the storyline
- ◆ using similes and metaphors
- ◆ using exaggeration
- ◆ using memorable phrasing
- ◆ how to present people in the writing
- ◆ how to use dialogue.

18.7.09

Extended writing

ones

In ~~threes~~, talk about any embarrassing incidents you have been involved in, such as:

◆ an embarrassing time on holiday

◆ a day you were in trouble at school

◆ an event with your own relatives.

Take it in turns to say what happened, quickly telling the story to the others. Now choose one of these events and use it as the opening for a piece of comic writing. Refer back to the hints you wrote down in the writing activity on page 21.

Write an account of the incident, making it humorous. See the funny side of it.

◆ Use a detached tone like Bill Bryson – as if you have stepped outside yourself to describe what is happening (e.g. 'My brain was telling me this was fine; my body didn't believe a word and just wanted to get out of there').

◆ Use a variety of sentences (including questions).

◆ Give details about people and places.

◆ Use dialogue to add humour.

Read your account aloud to other people. Talk about how you have each tried to create humour. Discuss the ways in which the written accounts feel different from the spoken versions with which you started the task.

What is autobiography?

Purpose and audience

Recounts tell readers about events that have happened. We have already seen them in newspapers and in personal accounts.

Autobiographies are important examples of recounts. They describe the events that have taken place in someone's own life. Usually, they will aim to entertain the reader.

Text level features

Most autobiography is written in a **chronological** sequence (placing events in the order in which they happened).

It is important to remember, however, that autobiographies often reflect the **personality** of the writer: they might change the conventions or rules of writing to suit themselves. For example, in his autobiography *Timebends*, the playwright Arthur Miller does not use a chronological sequence. Instead, he moves backwards and forwards over events in his life.

Sentence level features

Autobiographies use the **first person** ('I' and 'we'). They aim to paint a picture with words in order to help the reader visualize the scenes and events from the writer's life. **Connectives** like *then, later, next* will be used to link the ideas together and show the movement of time.

Word level features

Autobiographical writing will often use very descriptive language, and techniques such as **similes** and **metaphors**. It usually aims to answer the questions *who, what, where, when, why?*

Autobiographical recount
Healing the Horses

Learning objectives

In this extract, the writer gives an account of his own experiences in a form that reads like a novel. You will learn about the following objectives:

- Word level: work out unfamiliar words; recognize how a formal text needs appropriate word choice

- Sentence level: adapt text types for different purposes; understand differences between Standard English and dialects

- Reading: make notes in different ways; review your reading skills; look at changes when texts are adapted into different forms or media

- Writing: experiment with different approaches to planning, drafting and presenting writing; explain complex ideas and information; describe something using formal language where appropriate

Introduction

James Herriott's reflections on his career as a country vet became a huge hit when they were published in the 1970s, leading to a television series and a film.

They read like novels, but they are based largely on the vet's own real-life experiences. In this extract, he has been called out to look at some old shire horses. The name 'James Herriott' is part of the writer's technique – it is a character's name, not his real name, which he kept secret through to his retirement.

When you have studied the text, you will write a recount yourself.

Glossary

gelding – *male horse*

roan – *horse that has a coat sprinkled with white or grey*

venerable – *impressive and elderly*

excoriating – *removing skin from*

Healing the Horses

I was glad when we reached the flat land at the bottom. My arms seemed to have been stretched by several inches and I could feel a trickle of sweat on my brow. Old John appeared unaffected; he flicked the fork from his shoulder and the bale thudded on to the grass.

The two horses turned towards us at the sound. They were standing fetlock deep in the pebbly shallows just beyond a little beach which merged into the green carpet of turf; nose to tail, they had been rubbing their chins gently along each other's backs, unconscious of our approach. A high cliff overhanging the far bank made a perfect wind break while on either side of us clumps of oak blazed in the autumn sunshine.

'They're in a nice spot, Mr Skipton,' I said.

'Aye, they can keep cool in the hot weather and they've got the barn when winter comes.' John pointed to a low, thick-walled building with a single door. 'They can come and go as they please.'

The sound of his voice brought the horses out of the river at a stiff trot and as they came near you could see they really were old. The mare was a chestnut and the gelding was a light bay but their coats were so flecked with grey that they almost looked like roans. This was most pronounced on their faces where the sprinkling of white hairs, the sunken eyes and the deep cavity above the eyes gave them a truly venerable appearance.

For all that, they capered around John with a fair attempt at skittishness, stamping their feet, throwing their heads about, pushing his cap over his eyes with their muzzles.

'Get by, leave off!' he shouted. 'Daft awd beggars.' But he tugged absently at the mare's forelock and ran his hand briefly along the neck of the gelding.

'When did they last do any work?' I asked.

'Oh, about twelve years ago, I reckon.'

I stared at John. 'Twelve years! And have they been down here all that time?'

'Aye, just lakin' about down here, retired like. They've earned it an' all.' For a few moments he stood silent, shoulders hunched, hands deep in the pockets of his coat, then he spoke quietly as if to himself. 'They were two slaves when I was a slave.' He turned and looked at me and for a revealing moment I read in the pale blue eyes something of the agony and struggle he had shared with the animals.

'But twelve years! How old are they, anyway?'

John's mouth twisted up at one corner. 'Well you're t'vet. You tell me.'

I stepped forward confidently, my mind buzzing with Galvayne's groove, shape of marks, degree of slope and the rest; I grasped the unprotesting upper lip of the mare and looked at her teeth.

'Good God!' I gasped. 'I've never seen anything like this.' The incisors were immensely long and projecting forward till they met at an angle of about forty-five degrees. There were no marks at all – they had long since gone.

I laughed and turned back to the old man. 'It's no good, I'd only be guessing. You'll have to tell me.'

'Well she's about thirty and gelding's a year or two younger. She's had fifteen grand foals and never ailed owt except a bit of teeth trouble. We've had them rasped a time or two and it's time they were done again, I reckon. They're both losing ground and dropping bits of half chewed hay from their mouths. Gelding's the worst – has a right job champin' his grub.'

I put my hand into the mare's mouth, grasped her tongue and pulled it out to one side. A quick exploration of the molars with my other hand

revealed what I suspected; the outside edges of the upper teeth were overgrown and jagged and were irritating the cheeks while the inside edges of the lower molars were in a similar state and were slightly excoriating the tongue.

'I'll soon make her more comfortable, Mr Skipton. With those sharp edges rubbed off she'll be as good as new.' I got the rasp out of my vast box, held the tongue in one hand and worked the rough surface along the teeth, checking occasionally with my fingers till the points had been sufficiently reduced.

'That's about right,' I said after a few minutes. 'I don't want to make them too smooth or she won't be able to grind her food.'

John grunted. 'Good enough. Now have a look at t'other. There's summat far wrong with him.'

I had a feel at the gelding's teeth. 'Just the same as the mare. Soon put him right, too.'

But pushing at the rasp, I had an uncomfortable feeling that something was not quite right. The thing wouldn't go fully to the back of the mouth; something was stopping it. I stopped rasping and explored again, reaching with my fingers as far as I could. And I came upon something very strange, something which shouldn't have been there at all. It was like a great chunk of bone projecting down from the roof of the mouth.

It was time I had a proper look. I got out my pocket torch and shone it over the back of the tongue. It was easy to see the trouble now; the last upper molar was overlapping the lower one resulting in a gross overgrowth of the posterior border. The result was a sabre-like barb about three inches long stabbing down into the tender tissue of the gum.

That would have to come off – right now. My jauntiness vanished and I suppressed a shudder; it meant using the horrible shears – those great long-handled things with the screw operated by a cross bar. They gave me the willies because I am one of those people who can't bear to watch anybody blowing up a balloon and this was the same sort of thing only worse. You fastened the sharp blades of the shears on to the tooth and began to turn the bar slowly, slowly. Soon the tooth began to groan and creak under the tremendous leverage and you knew that any second it would break off and when it did it was like somebody letting off a rifle in your ear. That was when all hell usually broke loose but mercifully this was a quiet old horse and I wouldn't expect him to start dancing around on his hind legs. There was no pain for the horse because the overgrown part had no nerve supply – it was the noise that caused the trouble.

Returning to my crate I produced the dreadful instrument and with it a Haussman's gag which I inserted on the incisors and opened on its ratchet till the mouth gaped wide. Everything was easy to see then and, of course, there it was – a great prong at the other side of the mouth exactly like the first. Great, great, now I had two to chop off.

The old horse stood patiently, eyes almost closed, as though he had seen it all and nothing in the world was going to bother him. I went through the motions with my toes curling and when the sharp crack came, the white-bordered eyes opened wide, but only in mild surprise. He never even moved. When I did the other side he paid no attention at all; in fact, with the gag prising his jaws apart he looked exactly as though he was yawning with boredom.

As I bundled the tools away, John picked up the bony spicules from the grass and studied them with interest. 'Well, poor awd beggar. Good job I got you along, young man. Reckon he'll feel a lot better now.'

25. 7. 09.

UNDERSTANDING THE TEXT

Before examining the writer's techniques, look more closely at the facts in his account. You will need to read for meaning in different ways to do this.

1 How can you tell that the journey to reach the horses has been hard work for the narrator?

2 What signs are there that the horses are old?

3 How do the horses show that they like Mr Skipton?

4 What is the problem with the first horse's mouth?

5 What is the problem with the second horse's mouth?

INTERPRETING THE TEXT

Having looked at the facts in the text, now look at other meanings and at the writer's style.

6 Look at the men's conversation about how long it is since the horses last did any work. What is implied about Mr Skipton's past experiences, and his feelings for the horses?

7 What impression do you get of James Herriott from the extract? *The author* Think about:

   ◆ how he gets on with Mr Skipton

   ◆ how he deals with the horses' problems

   ◆ how he speaks.

8 The text is based on real-life people and events. But would it be possible to see it purely as a made-up story? What features do you notice in this autobiographical writing which you might also expect in fiction (for example, a novel set in the countryside)? Aim to find two features.

LANGUAGE AND STRUCTURE

1 While James Herriott speaks in Standard English, Mr Skipton uses a number of Yorkshire dialect words and structures.

   a Find a word he uses which we would not expect to find in Standard English.

   b Write down what you think the word means.

2 Now look again at James Herriott's own spoken words – such as: 'They're in a nice spot, Mr Skipton.' Which of the following statements do you think best explains the way the writer presents his own language?

   a The way James Herriott speaks shows that he comes from a different background from Mr Skipton.

   b It shows that James Herriott is an outsider in this area – he does not belong here.

   c James Herriott celebrates the way people speak in their own dialects.

   d James Herriott is presented as 'posh' in his language.

   Write a sentence explaining your choice.

3 Yorkshire dialect also uses certain phrases and structures, like these:
   retired like   an' all   t'other (rather than 'the other')

   Take the following three examples and write them in the Standard English dialect used by James Herriott:

   a 'Aye, just lakin' about down here, retired like.'

   b 'They've earned it an' all.'

   c 'Now have a look at t'other.'

4 Think about the way you have rewritten the dialect expressions in Standard English for question 3. Try to describe how you can tell the difference between Yorkshire dialect and Standard English. Use the list below to help you – it gives some examples of the ways different dialects may vary from Standard English.

   ◆ Irregular agreement between subject and verb (e.g. *we was*).

   ◆ Irregular formation of the past tense (e.g. it **were** finished).

- Different vocabulary from Standard English (e.g. *bairn* instead of *child*).

- Phrases which we would not find in Standard English.

- Different use of pronouns and prepositions (e.g. *we saw* **them** *horses*).

- Running two words of Standard English together to make a new word (e.g. *we saw* ***t'old*** *man*).

Start your comment like this:

Example a) seems like regional dialect rather than Standard English because …

WRITING ACTIVITY

James Herriott writes in a vivid personal style. How would his recount be different if it were a record of his work for the day, rather than an autobiography?

Imagine you are James Herriott and you have to keep a record of:

a the visits you make

b the problems the animals have

c the way you treat them.

Make some notes on the information you will include. Then write a short extract (one paragraph) for this record. Remember that the style will be more impersonal and less descriptive. You might start like this:

Thursday 23/8/01

Visit to Mr Skipton's farm. 2 old shire horses. Problem:

When you have finished, write a sentence or short paragraph describing the main similarities and differences between the style of your recount and James Herriott's autobiography.

Personal recount
Relative Values

Learning objectives

This extract gives a very personal view of a period in the writer's life. These are the objectives you will be studying:

- Word level: use prepositions and connectives; recognize how a formal text needs appropriate word choice

- Sentence level: look at the effect of different sentence structures; use a range of punctuation; link paragraphs

- Reading: follow themes and ideas; spot the difference between bias and objectivity

- Writing: present information clearly; describe something using formal language where appropriate

Introduction

Autobiography is an important type of text to consider when we are looking at recounts.

Many people think that autobiographical writing comes only in books describing a person's whole life. In fact, a lot of writing in newspapers, letters and journals is also autobiographical. It often focuses on one or two key moments from a writer's life.

The *Sunday Times* series 'Relative Values' does this. It invites people to talk about their relationship with a member of their family, and the way this has shaped who they are.

This example is written by the singer Des'ree. After looking at her recount, you can write one of your own.

Glossary

okra – *a tropical plant used as a vegetable*

apprehensive – *worried about what might happen*

antipathy – *the opposite of sympathy: rivalry and dislike*

Relative Values

I grew up in a happy household in southeast London. My parents appeared to be very happy together, there was lots of love and laughter, parties and music. My mum's laugh used to remind me of sunshine; it was always bright and crisp, and it used to touch me.

Dad was born in Barbados and came over here in the 1960s to study accountancy; my mother came over from Guyana at the same time to study nursing. My father was quiet, very reserved, and left most things up to my mother, who was highly ambitious and wanted the best for her family. She really pushed and encouraged my father. That was a pattern in his life. He had very domineering parents. As a boy he was a talented cricketer – Sir Gary Sobers came to his school and asked the headmaster if he could play for the West Indies. But his parents felt cricket wasn't a stable occupation, that he should be academic and go to university, and wouldn't allow it.

Dad's main loves in life when I was a child were cricket and jazz. Every Saturday he would get together with his West Indian friends and cook traditional West Indian food, particularly *coucou*,

which is the national dish of Barbados, a stew of cornmeal and okra served with flying fish. It was a ritual my Dad loved; there would be jazz music in the background, and they'd talk all night about cricket and make jokes, and it kept up his links with his homeland.

After my parents had lived in Britain for 20 years, they wanted my sister and me to experience the West Indies, so we upped sticks and moved to Barbados. My dad seemed happy and relaxed there, meeting his old buddies, and of course he fitted straight in because it was the country of his birth and his relatives were there. My mum was a little more apprehensive. We lived in my father's parents' home, which she was never really happy about, and they weren't very keen on my mum, to be honest, because she wasn't from the island. It's the small-island, big-island thing – there is a natural antipathy between the Bajans and the Guyanans.

So Mum wanted to have her own home, and she put pressure on my dad to find somewhere else for us to live, but he saw no reason to move from the family home. He felt it was big enough,

he was happy there – basically, any excuse. Meanwhile, I noticed that the happy times in our family unit were becoming much more rare. There was less talk. Then there was no talking at all. My parents didn't pretend everything was okay – my mother has always been very open. She said: 'Daddy and I are going through a difficult period, but don't be alarmed by it, this is what happens sometimes within a marriage, and you have to work things through.'

I suppose my sister and I didn't really take in what was happening because at the end of the day we felt, that's adult business, they'll deal with it, because parents take care of everything. But I remember looking at my father after that conversation, and I looked at him in a different way. He was always so quiet, I thought: 'What's going on in your mind? Why don't you throw a tantrum, *do* something, Daddy!' My attitude towards him changed then, because I saw he was weak, and we don't expect our parents to be weak, we expect them to be pillars of strength. So I started to feel jittery, because I knew that the link, the connection, was about to be

31

severed, and when I felt things starting to crumble it tore me apart.

He retreated. He found it very difficult to talk to us. It could have been guilt, it could have been a number of things, but I stopped communicating with him then because he had become like a stranger to me.

One day Mum sat us down in the kitchen. 'Your father and I are no longer going to be together,' she said. 'We're going to get a divorce.' She was very composed then, because she wanted to be

composed for us. My sister and I burst out crying, there were lots of tears. But I was the eldest, and I realised I had to step into my dad's position. I had to be the strong one, because I wouldn't want Mum to think there was nobody there for her.

Dad stayed in the house until it was time for us to go back to England. I can remember saying goodbye to him; it was like looking at a stranger. I remember my sister and my mother crying, but I didn't shed a tear, and I was angry at them for crying. Maybe that was just my way of coping. I was like a pillar of steel, I refused to be moved by the whole thing and detached myself. In a way, I felt sorry for him because I thought: 'We're going to be okay, but I don't know what's going to happen to you.'

Dad stayed on in the Caribbean. My mother always encouraged us to keep in contact, either by phone or by letter, which I did for her sake – not for my own, because I was still angry. It was 10 years later when my father came to London. We went to see him at the airport, and I was surprised by how much he had changed. We were shocked at his appearance: he looked so much older, he seemed very

weary. He wouldn't really convey anything to us. 'Oh, I'm fine,' he said, 'a little trouble with my eyes and my blood pressure.' But that was it. Nothing deeper.

The most significant time I've spent with my father was when my sister and I went to St Lucia on holiday with him last Christmas. We were together for five weeks and we were finally able to talk to him. My sister is a psychologist, so she was able to extract things from him that I couldn't, and it was as though I was getting to know him for the first time – his likes, his dislikes, his goals, his dreams, his fears.

I didn't hold back. I said how angry we were, how rejected we had felt, I just kind of laid it out. He took it quietly; maybe he hadn't anticipated that I would tell him that. Not that everything is happy ever after, because he wasn't able to balm those wounds. But I'm not angry any more. I realise now that my father was one of those people who are too easy-going. He regretted not playing for the West Indies cricket team, he regretted certain other opportunities in his life he didn't take because he didn't have the guts to jump in and take the risk, and that included the marriage.

1. 8. 09.

UNDERSTANDING THE TEXT

1 Write down two facts we learn from the article about her parents' background – one about Des'ree's mother and another about her father.

2 Why did the family move to Barbados?

3 Why did the father's family not get on with Des'ree's mother?

4 How did Des'ree's attitude to her father change in Barbados?

5 When did Des'ree last see her father?

INTERPRETING THE TEXT

6 How can you tell that Des'ree's family is important to her?

7 By the end of the article she says: 'I'm not angry any more.' How has her understanding of her father changed? Can we see this change developing as her recount goes along?

8 How would you describe the tone of the writer?

bitter   angry   disappointed   resentful   accepting

Write down the word that you think is most suitable, and then write a sentence explaining why you have chosen it.

9 Some people might say that Des'ree's recount seems biased rather than factual – that it is impossible for her to describe her life and family in an objective way. Do you agree or disagree? Say why.

10 Personal recounts tend to contain both facts and opinions. Use a table like the one below to sort out the differences between facts and opinions in this text.

Facts about her father	Opinions about her father
Facts about her mother	Opinions about her mother
Facts about Des'ree	

Why don't we gain any direct opinions of Des'ree herself?

LANGUAGE AND STRUCTURE

1 Some parts of Des'ree's text feel quite formal; other parts seem informal.

a Find three examples of formal words or phrases and three of informal ones. Try to explain why you think they are formal or informal. An example is done for you.

Formal style

Example: *there is a natural antipathy*

Comment: ***antipathy*** *is an unfamiliar, technical word.*

Informal style

Example: *so we upped sticks and moved to Barbados*

Comment: ***upped sticks*** *is a chatty expression which you might use in spoken English rather than a written text.*

b The writer refers to her parents as 'Mum' and 'Dad'. What effect would it have if she used the phrases 'my mother' and 'my father' instead?

2 Des'ree uses a variety of sentences and joins them together with connectives. Her recount moves backwards and forwards in time. At the start of some paragraphs she uses connectives to help the reader follow the sequence of her writing.

Look at these three examples of connectives used at the beginning of paragraphs, and describe the purpose of each one. Use the prompt list on the next page to help you.

Example of connective	Purpose of the connective
After (paragraph 4)	
So (paragraph 5)	
One day (paragraph 8)	

Possible purposes of connectives

- to move us back in time

- to give an illustration or example

- to show the effect of something that has happened

- to move us forward in time

- to summarize or generalize

- to move to a different setting.

3 Look at the two examples below, where Des'ree uses semi-colons within her sentences:

Dad was born in Barbados and came over here in the 1960s to study accountancy; my mother came over from Guyana at the same time to study nursing.

He took it quietly; maybe he hadn't anticipated that I would tell him that.

a How would the effect have been different if Des'ree had used a full stop instead of the semi-colon?

b How does the semi-colon help Des'ree to express her meaning more precisely?

WRITING ACTIVITY

Although the text is chiefly about Des'ree and her feelings, we also learn quite a lot about her parents. Imagine you are Des'ree's father. Retell some of the text from his point of view. Structure it like this:

- your background and early life in Britain

- why you decided to return to Barbados

- how you felt that things went wrong

- how you feel now about your relationship with Des'ree.

Aim to show the father's point of view, helping the reader to understand what he is like. Remember to use the first person, set events in chronological order, link your ideas with connectives, and use descriptive words to help your reader visualize the scenes.

Extended writing

Write a short piece for your own autobiography. You might choose a comic scene, when something funny happened to you, or a moving one, like Des'ree's.

Start by making notes on the moment you will describe. These might include:

◆ describing a place where you used to live

◆ recalling memories of parents or a friend

◆ recounting an incident that happened at school.

Brainstorm details of people, places, time, and any colours, smells or other fragments of memory you have.

Think about how personal your style will be. Then plan how you will organize your autobiographical writing. Will you use chronological order, or move backwards and forwards in time?

Think of connectives you might use to link sentences and paragraphs into a clear sequence for readers to follow.

Aim to produce 3 to 5 paragraphs of concentrated autobiographical writing.

Information texts: the essentials

Purpose and audience

Information texts describe how things are. They might include reference books, dictionaries, textbooks, factsheets, and leaflets.

The audience will be people who want to know more about the topic. They may already have some knowledge of the subject.

Information texts will be clear, well-ordered, and easy to follow.

Text level features

Information texts will often use **headings** to break the information up into different sections, and use **layout features** such as tables and diagrams to help make the information clear.

They might start with **general facts** and then go into more **detail**. Often they use a **non-chronological order** – they place information in order of importance, not the order that events take place.

Sentence level features

Information texts will usually use:

♦ the **third-person** form, to create an impersonal tone

♦ the **present tense**

♦ the **passive voice** ('salmon are farmed in large tanks' rather than 'people farm salmon in large tanks')

♦ a mix of **simple and compound sentences**

♦ **questions** addressed to the reader, to involve the reader more.

Word level features

Information texts will often use very precise terms, and sometimes **technical language**. This will depend on how much the writer thinks the reader knows about the topic. The writers of information texts avoid using much descriptive language. They will emphasize **facts**, using nouns and verbs in order to describe processes, and the text will usually be formal.

Technical information
Exploded Drawings

Learning objectives

This extract explains some technical information and uses specialist vocabulary. These are the objectives you will be studying:

- Word level: work out unfamiliar words; explain what words mean in particular places; recognize how a formal text needs appropriate word choice

- Sentence level: look at different sentence structures; explore ways of grouping sentences into paragraphs; know how to write in a form to suit a particular subject; explore different levels of formality in different texts

- Reading: combine information from different sources; use a range of reading skills for research; make notes in different ways; review your reading skills; follow themes and ideas; spot the difference between bias and objectivity; explore implied and explicit meanings; look at how meaning changes when texts are adapted to different forms; recognize how texts are shaped by the technology they use

- Writing: present information clearly; explain complex ideas; describe something using formal language where appropriate

- Speaking and listening: listen for a specific purpose

Introduction

Information texts are often aimed at people who know something about a subject, but may need to find out more. These texts are often designed to be used for reference – for those times when you need to look for more information about a topic or process. This means that clarity is most important. The best information texts don't use just language to inform the reader – they will use layout too.

This page from a textbook used by students studying Design Technology is about 'exploded drawings'. Examine the way it presents information. It is aimed at an audience aged 15 to 16. When you have studied this text, you can practise presenting the information yourself.

6.4 EXPLODED DRAWINGS

BY THE END OF THIS SPREAD, YOU SHOULD BE ABLE TO:

ʌ produce exploded drawings

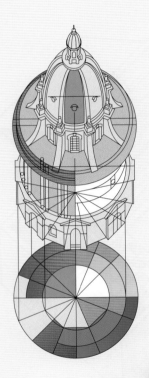

Illustration 4 .

Exploded drawings help the designer or manufacturer explain to the user how a product is assembled.

Exploded drawings are three-dimensional drawings. They are usually drawn using perspective.

It is important that the drawings of the individual parts of a product are separated so that the viewer can easily mentally assemble them. If the exploded parts are too close together or too far apart, it becomes more difficult to do this.

Illustrations 1, 2 & 3 show three exploded illustrations of three familiar components – a bolt, a washer and a nut. Which illustration do you think would be most helpful to a young child assembling the three parts?

We can also produce vertically drawn exploded views of the same components (Illustration 4).

The following illustration has been drawn using a different exploded drawing method.

Illustration 1

Illustration 2

Illustration 3

As you can see, it is useful to 'raise the roof' of a building to allow the viewer to look inside. This exposes aspects of the interior planning or layout.

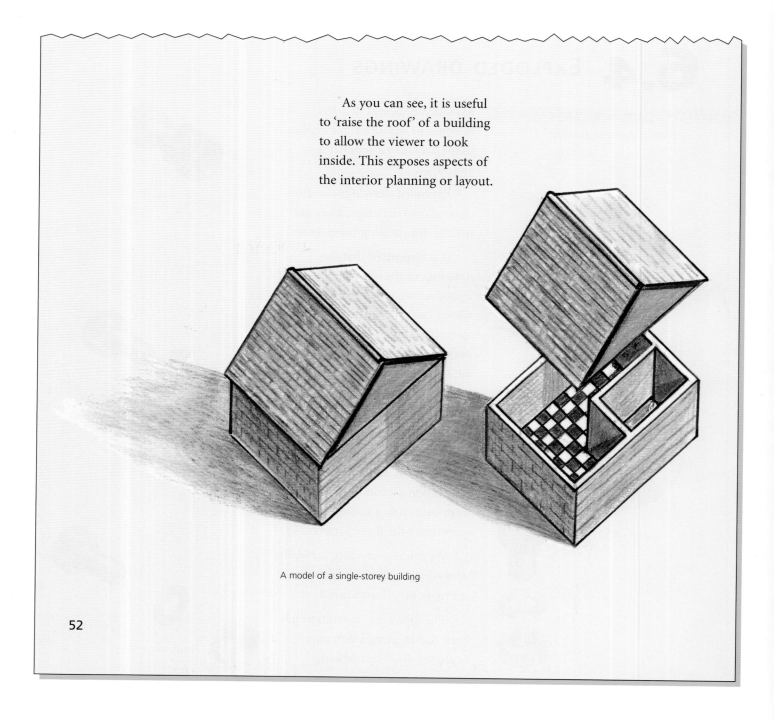

A model of a single-storey building

52

8.8.09.   WEEK① 1-8

UNDERSTANDING THE TEXT

1 What is an exploded drawing for?

2 How does the writer help readers to know what they should have learned by the end of the unit?

3 Why do the drawings need to show the separate parts of objects?

4 Look at the formal words below. Think of a different word or phrase that the writer might have used for:

  a how a product is **assembled**

  b views of the same **components**.

INTERPRETING THE TEXT

5 In information texts, paragraphs are often organized so that each contains one piece of information. Look at the structure of this text. It is written in short paragraphs. Use a grid like the one below to say what each of these paragraphs is about.

Paragraph	Topic
1	
2	
3	
4	
5	

6 Using your completed grid to help you, decide which of these statements (a–d) you most agree with.

  a The text gives a lot of examples of exploded drawings.

  b The text starts with an example of an exploded drawing, and then shows how these can work in other subject areas.

  c The first paragraph introduces the topic. The second gives more detail. The rest of the paragraphs provide examples.

d The first paragraph introduces the topic. Paragraphs 2 and 3 give more information. Paragraph 4 gets the reader thinking about examples. Paragraph 5 gives a further example.

Write a sentence explaining your choice.

7 On a scale of 1 (low) to 5 (high), how helpful do you find the layout of the page in making the information clear? Write a sentence saying how you think the layout could be improved.

8 Think about the audience for this text. Is it aimed at people who know very little about the subject, people who have a background understanding, or experts? Write a sentence explaining how you can tell.

LANGUAGE AND STRUCTURE

1 Working with a partner, tell her or him about the information you have read in this text. Your partner should make notes about the way you describe the information.

In particular, listen out for:

♦ informal words

♦ longer sentences than are used in the book

♦ fillers (*er, erm*) and repetition – these are known as **non-fluency features**.

2 Like many information texts, this textbook uses quite formal language. It includes some technical words: *perspective, three-dimensional, exploded, interior.*

a Choose one of these technical terms and – using your own words – write down what you think it means.

b Describe something the writer might have done to help a reader who does *not* know that word.

3 Information texts tend to be written mostly in statements. This text includes a question:

Which illustration do you think would be ...?

Why do you think the writer includes a question at this point?

4 Look at this sentence:

The following illustration <u>has been drawn</u> using a different exploded drawing method.

  a The writer has written this in the passive voice. He or she could have written it in the active voice using the pronoun 'we'. Write an active version of the sentence, starting with 'We'.

  b Why do you think the writer chose the passive form?

WRITING ACTIVITY

Imagine a friend has written to you to say that she or he is stuck with Design homework. Write a letter back, explaining about the topic of exploded drawings. Remember to use the present tense, and to use words that give a precise meaning, rather than general description. Use headings and sub-headings if you wish.

- How will you structure the information differently?
- How will you address the reader differently?
- How will you use vocabulary and sentences differently?

Write a short paragraph comparing your version with the original.

Unit 3

Extended writing

Look at the list of facts below about Florence Nightingale. Your task is to inform Year 7 students about the key facts of her life.

Think about the way you will organize the information.

- How will you use layout features to help the reader?
- What types of sentences will you use (simple, compound, complex)?
- Will you use questions as well as statements?
- Will you use the third person?
- How will you address the reader?
- Will you use the past or present tense?

Florence Nightingale

- Born 1820, died 1910.
- A British hospital reformer and founder of the modern nursing profession.
- She had strong religious convictions.
- She trained as a nurse, and was appointed a nursing superintendent in London in 1853.
- On the outbreak of the Crimean War, in 1854, she volunteered to lead a party of nurses to work in the military hospitals in Scutari, Turkey.
- She set about transforming the appalling conditions. The death rate was reduced from 42% to 2%.
- She earned the nickname 'The Lady with the Lamp'.
- In 1856 she founded Florence Nightingale School and Home for nurses in London.
- She wrote a classic book called *Notes on Nursing*.
- She was awarded the Order of Merit in 1907 – a high award.

You might start by sketching out what your page will look like. You don't need to draw any pictures – just draw a box and write a label saying what the picture would show.

Explanation texts: the essentials

Purpose and audience

Explanation texts explain how things work and why things happen. They give us the answers to questions (such as 'Why did war break out in 1914?') and they are usually clear and direct.

Text level features

Explanation texts will often:

* use **layout features** to make their explanation clearer (e.g. questions, sub-headings, boxes, illustrations, diagrams, maps)
* begin with a general **opening statement** ('Europe in 1914 was on the brink of war …')
* give a **step-by-step** account of an event or process
* end with a **summary**.

Sentence level features

Explanation texts usually:

* use the **third-person** form to create an impersonal tone
* use the **present tense** (in science and technical writing, for example) or the **past tense** (for historical writing)
* make some use of the **passive voice** to keep the tone impersonal ('the potassium was then added to the solution')
* use a mix of **simple and compound sentences**
* use **connectives** to show how one idea relates to another and to indicate cause and effect (e.g. *after, until, later*).

Word level features

Explanation texts often use very precise terms, and sometimes **technical language**. This will depend on how much the writer thinks the reader knows about the topic. Explanation texts usually avoid using much descriptive language – they will emphasize **facts**. They use nouns and verbs in order to describe processes.

Explaining a process
Why is the sky blue most of the time but can be red at sunset and sunrise?

Learning objectives

This website page gives an easy-to-follow explanation of what is happening during a process. These are the objectives you will be studying:

- Word level: understand what words mean in particular contexts; use a range of prepositions and connectives; recognize how the formality of a text influences your choice of words

- Sentence level: explore changes in tense; understand the use of conditionals and modal verbs; know how to write in specific forms in particular subjects; identify key changes when a text is changed from informal to formal

- Reading: follow themes and ideas

- Writing: organize and present information clearly

Introduction

Most explanation texts answer a question. The text in this unit is taken from the BBC Science Shack website. In it, scientist Adam Hart-Davis answers online questions. To explain science to his audience he uses a mixture of instructions (how to do an experiment) and explanation (showing how the experiment works). He also gives some information about the history of the experiment.

After you have studied this explanation text, you will be able to write one of your own.

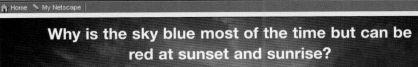

BBC Online – Science – Science Shack – Make – Netscape 6

http://www.bbc.co.uk/science/scienceshack/experiments/mabluesky.shtml ▾ Search

🏠 Home ✎ My Netscape

Why is the sky blue most of the time but can be red at sunset and sunrise?

Question asked by Martin Glaister

Why the sky is blue was first discovered by John Tyndall, a clever scientist who succeeded Michael Faraday as director of the Royal Institution in 1867. Tyndall was very good at thinking up demonstrations, and even thought up a way of making his own blue sky. Have a go yourself and see how it works.

What you need:

Fish tank   Torch   Wooden block or books
Dried milk powder   Teaspoon

What to do:

Start by filling the fish tank with water and then balance the torch on the wooden block so that it is shining down the length of the tank. Next add about a quarter teaspoon of milk powder and give it a good stir. Now look at the side of the tank – the water should look slightly blue. This is your sky; it is not very blue, as it is only a very little sky. Look at the end of the fish tank and you should see a yellow sun, your torch. Keep adding milk, a quarter teaspoon at a time, and watch your sky get bluer and your sun turn reddish, like at sunset.

How it works:

Tyndall noticed that when you shone a torch, you could often see the beam. But when he tried this with clean filtered air, he saw nothing at all. He realised that the only reason that you can 'see' beams of light is that the air is full of tiny particles of dust that scatter the light. And this is exactly what is happening in your fish tank. When a ray of light hits a milk particle it bounces off in all directions – the light is scattered. Small particles scatter blue light more than red. This means that when you look at the scattered light from the side of the tank, it is slightly blue, but when you look at the end of the tank you see the rest of the spectrum – mostly yellow and red. So the sky is blue because it is full of tiny floating particles of dust that scatter the blue parts of sunlight. In turn the sun gets redder at sunset as the light travels through more atmosphere, so more light is scattered and only red gets through. Bizarrely, if the air above us were absolutely clear of dust and water, the sky would be black.

Document: Done

Business ▲ Tech ▲ Fun ▲ Interact ▲

UNDERSTANDING THE TEXT

1 Pick out two sentences from the text which you think best answer the question asked by Martin Glaister.

2 What was the relationship of John Tyndall to Michael Faraday?

3 What was Tyndall particularly good at?

INTERPRETING THE TEXT

4 How does Adam Hart-Davis use layout to make his explanation easy to follow?

5 How might the writing itself have been made easier to follow? If you had been the editor of the page, would you have added bullet points, shorter paragraphs, more sub-headings, words in bold or italics? Write a brief paragraph about how you might make the explanation even clearer.

6 Why do you think Adam Hart-Davis includes historical information about John Tyndall?

7 By the end of the text, do you feel that the original question has been fully answered? Are there any further questions it makes you want to ask?

LANGUAGE AND STRUCTURE

1 Adam Hart-Davis uses a number of sentence functions in his text. Find an example of:

 ◆ a command

 ◆ a statement.

2 a Write down a phrase or sentence in which Adam Hart-Davis uses the past tense.

 b Write down a phrase or sentence in which Adam Hart-Davis uses the present tense.

3 The text is structured like this:

   1 introduction

   2 ingredients

   3 instruction

   4 explanation

   a Why is section 1 written mostly in the past tense?

   b Why is the last sentence of section 1 in the present tense?

   c Why is section 3 in the present tense?

   d Why does section 4 start in the past and then change to the present tense?

4 Look at the instructions in section 3. Write down two connectives the writer uses to show that one instruction follows another.

5 Explanation texts can be written in quite an informal tone. Adam Hart-Davis does this in two main ways.

   a He addresses the reader directly, like this:

     *This means that when **you** look at the scattered light from the side of the tank, it is slightly blue ...*

     Write this sentence so that it is more formal and does not refer directly to the reader.

   b He also uses some informal vocabulary, like this:

     *When a ray of light **hits** a milk particle it **bounces off in all directions** ...*

     Try to write this in a more formal, technical style, by paying particular attention to the highlighted words.

   c Why do you think Adam Hart-Davis chooses this informal tone?

6 The last section of the text explains how something works. It uses a number of connectives to show how one idea relates to another. Look at the list of connectives on the next page and describe what part each one plays in the text. The first example is done for you.

Connective	Function
And	Shows how this idea continues from the last one
This means	
So	
In turn	
If	

7 Look at the way the writer uses verbs:

Look at the end of the fish tank and you **should** *see a yellow sun …*

How would the effect be different if he had said *you will, might,* or *could* see?

a Which of these modal verbs feels *most* definite?

b Which feels *least* definite?

8 How would you redesign the page to make the process clearer for a younger audience? How would you use images differently? Would you organize the text in a different way?

Map out a new page design for the website. Then write a brief paragraph explaining why your changes would make the information easier for a young reader to understand.

WRITING ACTIVITY

The extract we have studied here is an explanation of a process that you might explore in a science lesson. How does writing differ in the various subjects you study at school? Use the questions below to reflect on the way you are expected to write. Then put together some writing hints for other students.

Writing survey

- The subject that requires the most writing from me is …
- The subject that requires the least writing from me is …
- The subject that requires the most formal style is …
- The subject that encourages the most detail in my writing is …
- The subject that requires the least description is …

Writing hints

If you were giving advice to a new student on how to produce the best writing in one subject area, what would you say?

Choose one subject and, using these prompts, think of three to five hints you would give for each.

Subject:
Hints on the kinds of words to use (e.g. how technical, how informal, how much description?) ▲ ▲ ▲
Hints on the kinds of sentences (e.g. simple, complex, mostly questions/statements/commands) ▲ ▲ ▲
Hints on how to set out writing (e.g. notes, long paragraphs, bullet points, sub-headings)

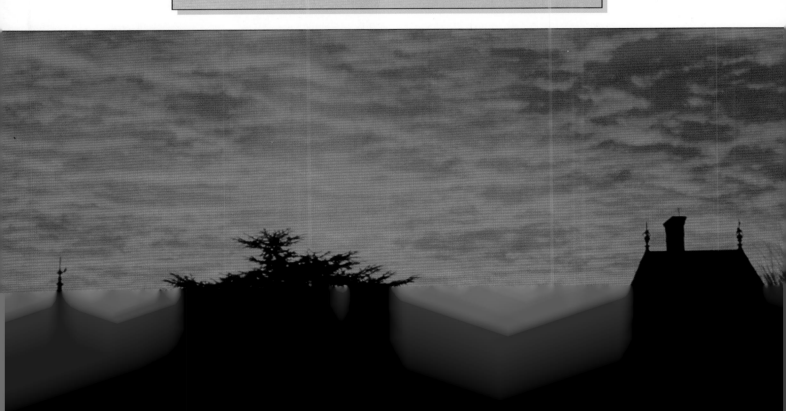

Unit 4

Extended writing

Choose a process you know well. Write an explanation for a general reader. Possible topics might include:

- How your school day is organized.
- Why people play the national lottery.
- How the gears on a bike work.
- How a computer spellchecker works.

Make notes of the key points first, then write your explanation, using the third person and the present tense, with connectives to show how one idea relates to another.

Assess Your Learning

Unit 1 Personal recounts

Work with a partner to review the work you produced for the writing activity on page 21.

1 With your partner, read your work carefully and look for evidence of the skills listed in the chart below. Copy the chart and record examples from your own work.

Formal writing skills	Examples	My progress
Use a detached tone		◯
Use a variety of sentences		◯
Give details about people and places		◯
Use dialogue to add humour		◯

2 Now assess your work. Decide with your partner which traffic light best matches your progress so far and colour it in the chart.

⬤ I find this difficult to do.　◯ I'm doing quite well at this, but not all the time.　◯ I'm doing well at this.

3 Look at the skills you have labelled yellow or red. Decide two skills to target next time you write a formal information text.

Unit 2 Autobiographical recounts

1 a In Unit 2 you read two different types of autobiographical recount, one by James Herriot and the other by Des'ree. Based on your reading, what would you say are three essential features in good autobiographical writing?

b Share your ideas to compile a class list. Then decide, as a class, which are the three most important features.

c Look back at your own work and identify where you have used these features. Which have you used least and could target next time you write an autobiographical recount?

2 Look at the work you produced for the writing activity on page 35. Find examples of different types of connectives, listed in the grid below. If any are missing, can you see opportunities where you might have used them effectively?

Types of connective	Example of use/opportunity to use
To move back in time	
To give an example or illustration	
To show the effect of something	
To move forward in time	
To summarize or generalize	
To move to a different setting	

Unit 3 Information texts

In this unit, you have given verbal information about exploded drawings to a partner and written a letter giving information on the topic.

  a With a partner, think carefully about each task you performed, and make notes under these headings: the planning I did; the description skills I used; how I checked the information I was giving was making sense; how I revised my description; how I used the plan.

  b Which task did you find easiest to do and why?

  c What would you do differently next time?

Unit 4 Explanation texts

1 a Look back at your response to Adam Hart-Davis's explanation about why the sky turns red at sunrise and sunset. Tick the reading strategies that you used to help you understand the text. Add another strategy that you find effective when reading a complex explanation.

  b What else do you think the writer could have included or done differently to make the explanation clearer to a reader?

2 Look at your work for the extended writing task on page 52. Create a spider diagram with the words 'Writing to explain' in the centre. Around the title note four or five features of your work that show you have understood how to explain ideas clearly to your reader. Focus on really specific points by looking back at the learning objectives at the start of the unit.

Reading strategies	Tick or cross
Skimming headings	
Scanning text for key words	
Reading forwards	
Rereading text	
Looking up unfamiliar words	
Visualizing what the writer is saying (using the writer's words to build up a picture in the mind)	

Getting started

Unit 5 Writing to persuade

1 The topics below are the kind of motions that are sometimes set for debates:

- Eating meat is wrong.
- Violence is never justified.
- Censoring the Internet is a good idea.
- School sports should be increased to three hours a week.
- Sweets, crisps and fizzy drinks should be banned in schools.

Working with a partner, choose one topic and think of three arguments FOR and three arguments AGAINST the motion.

2 If you were writing an article in a magazine to put your point of view about your chosen topic, you would want to catch your reader's interest immediately. You could start with:

- a story
- an unusual fact
- a quotation.
- a statistic
- a vivid description

Think of two or three possible opening sentences to grab your reader's attention. Decide which one is best and be ready to share it with the rest of the class.

Unit 6 Advice texts

1 How good are you at giving and receiving advice? Imagine a friend of yours has bought a new outfit and asks what you think about it. Would you:

a tell her or him directly that you don't like it?

b find a polite way to hint that you're not keen?

c avoid giving your opinion?

2 Look at option (b). With two friends, role-play how you might approach this situation. Two of you should be the friends and one of you should listen to the language that is used.

How does the speaker use language to tell the friend about her or his opinion? How does she or he try to avoid upsetting the listener?

3 As a class, make a summary of at least three techniques that people use to give advice effectively.

Unit 7 Writing analysis

When we do an analysis we try to show how something works, or why one product is better than another. It often means avoiding a personal opinion by using factual evidence.

1 With a partner, choose two products you both know well. For example: a movie and its sequel; two rival brands of soft drink; two music download websites; two types of MP3 player.

  a Discuss in detail which product is better. Try to avoid just giving your opinion, and instead provide some evidence:
  - For films: comment on the acting, editing, pace of the story, depth of the characterization, quality of the special effects
  - Soft drinks: comment on the packaging, what the taste reminds you of, the level of sweetness, the depth of flavour, the after-taste
  - Websites: comment on the overall design, navigation features, ease of use, clarity, range of features, number of links and irritating pop-up windows
  - MP3 players: comment on the design, portability, ease of use, battery life, clarity of music, additional features.

  b How easy or difficult was it to have this analytical conversation? Did you manage to provide enough evidence to support your views?

Unit 8 Writing reviews

1 Play *Desert Island Books*. If you were shipwrecked on a desert island, which one book would you like to have with you? Consider:
- picture books
- books that you read when you were learning to read
- the first books you read on your own
- class readers you have specially enjoyed.

Choose one key book and prepare to say:
- what the book is about
- what you remember about when you first read it
- why you particularly like it.

2 Write down a summary of your book recommendation and add it to a class display of *The Books that Changed our Lives*.

Persuasive writing: the essentials

Purpose and audience

Persuasive writing aims to:

◆ express a point of view
◆ change your opinions
◆ get you to buy something.

Text types used for persuasive writing include letters, essays, advertisements, leaflets, television programmes, newspaper editorials and opinion pieces. Writers will use language and structures intended to make you see things from their point of view.

Text level features

◆ The text may use **illustrations** to help get its points across.

◆ It may use **layout features** – such as font sizes – for impact.

◆ The writing may start with an **opening statement**, and then go through **key points** in more detail.

◆ **Logical links** will guide readers through the points made.

◆ The writer may use **humour** to catch the reader's interest.

Sentence level features

◆ The writer may use the **first person** (I, we) to express opinions, or may write using the **third person** (she, he, they) for a more impersonal effect.

◆ Advertising might use the **second person** and **imperatives** (commands) to create a more direct appeal.

◆ Persuasive writing will usually use **active** rather than passive sentence structures, and is often written in the **present tense**.

Word level features

◆ **Emotive words** may be chosen to try to influence the reader, and sometimes **exaggerated language**.

◆ In advertising, writers may use **word play** for effect.

Getting your point across

It's For You

Learning objectives

This newspaper article gives a teacher's opinions on mobile phones. You will be studying the following objectives:

- Word level: recognize how the formality of a text influences your choice of words

- Sentence level: look at the impact of sentence structures; explore changes in tense; identify key changes when a text is changed from informal to formal

- Reading: distinguish between bias and objectivity

- Writing: present a case persuasively; develop and signpost arguments

- Speaking and listening: use talk to question, hypothesize and speculate; recognize and build on others' contributions; explore ideas through role-play

Introduction

Here is an opinion piece by a teacher at a sixth form college. She wrote this article in a newspaper aimed at new teachers. Her purpose is to show the effects mobile phones can have on your lessons if you are a teacher. See whether you think she presents a persuasive argument. When you have studied this text, you can write a persuasive article of your own.

Glossary

winsome – *pleasing or attractive*

26.9.09

It's for you

The mobile phone is a menace to even the best-planned class. Cassandra Hilland has heard one bleep too many

Imagine it's your first proper lesson. It has to go well. You worry you'll be scarred for life if it doesn't. So you've planned and agonised over acetates, dithered over delivery, and decided that your bum does look big in your new trouser suit. Finally, you're ready (you hope). It's 9am, time for the first lesson of the rest of your life.

By 9.20, you're in full flow. Your punchy opening grabbed their interest. Your pitch was spot on. Now you're gliding through your audio-visuals with the winsome grace of a weather girl. As you remember their names and ask questions, you think you're the best teacher in the stratosphere. Now you're going to deconstruct Hamlet's language. You fix the class with an intense stare: 'Right then. Let us consider the character of this complex individual.' (God you're good!) 'What do you think Hamlet meant by his last words: "The rest is silence?" Hmmmm?'

You pause for dramatic effect. Then a mobile phone starts to bleep. While you try to recapture your lost chain of thought, every student in the class rummages in pockets and bags. Before they were focused, now they're wriggling in their seats. You have changed from Impressive Teacher into Flailing Failure in nanoseconds.

The lesson is trashed. All you can hear are giggles and a tacky rendition of 'Greensleeves'. Forget what they told you about disruptive pupils – the real threat to discipline is the mobile phone.

My response is to paste a large sign on my classroom door requesting that mobile phones be switched off before entering. The day after the warning goes up, a pulse trills from a girl's bag. I snarl. 'It's okay,' she reassures me. 'It's my pager, not my mobile!' The class laughs uneasily. I wince. What other digital demons have I left out? This may cause amusement, but it is a waste of teaching time.

These communication aids actually achieve the opposite. They not only distract but initiate battles of one-upmanship and anti-social behaviour. There we are discussing poetry when, suddenly, the affable young chap who's just been so articulate on symbolism has turned his back and is grunting into a plastic box. Worse is the bizarre status students attach to mobiles. Students even assert their group identity through a chosen make and model. For example, there's a chrome Samsung number which is so expensive that any student who owns one is sending out a clear signal to their peers.

The student mobile phone user is a sign of changing times. I don't understand voice dialling, or press-on covers, and most of these little gimmicks are harmless. But there are some altogether more sinister aspects to mobile phone use that are only just being uncovered.

Text message bullying is a problem. So is cheating. Now that the latest phones can access the Internet, students can search for answers. Perhaps we will have to frisk tomorrow's students for gadgets before they sit their exams. Or use an airport-style sensor at the exam hall door.

In the absence of any solution in the battle to stop students using mobiles in the classroom, I suggest the following: lay down the law from day one. Get your students into the habit of switching off phones, pagers and car alarms before they enter the classroom. You could even have a fish tank of piranhas on your desk, with some fluorescent-fronted phones at the bottom as a thought-provoking decoration.

As for me, I've taken the ultimate precaution – lining my classroom walls with lead.

UNDERSTANDING THE TEXT

1 Look at the first paragraph. Who do you think the writer is addressing here?

2 What words and phrases in paragraph 2 suggest that the imaginary lesson is going well?

3 Look at paragraph 4: 'Forget what they told you about disruptive pupils …'. Who do you think 'they' refers to?

4 What does the writer mean by 'the bizarre status pupils attach to mobile phones' (paragraph 6)?

5 What is the writer's advice for dealing with mobile phones in class?

INTERPRETING THE TEXT

6 What impression do you gain of the writer's personality from the text? Give reasons for your answer.

7 Persuasive texts often include humour. How does this writer use humour to make her points? Look for examples of:

- ◆ deliberate exaggeration
- ◆ poking fun at teachers and pupils
- ◆ comic phrases
- ◆ telling a story.

8 Some readers may feel that the writer is not objective enough – that she makes **assertions** (opinionated comments) without supporting them with evidence. Is this true? Find an example from the text as evidence for your view.

9 Which parts of the writer's article do you agree with? Which do you disagree with? Working in pairs or a small group, argue the case for and against pupils having mobile phones in school. Try to come up with a list of arguments for and against their use. You could do this in role – one of you playing the part of a pupil, another a parent, another a teacher, another could be someone from a mobile phone company.

half a
page

LANGUAGE AND STRUCTURE

1 a Look at the way the writer uses the first-person (*I* and *we*)
and the second-person (*you*) forms to give her opinion.
Which paragraphs use the first person and which use the second?

Paragraph	First or second person?
1: 'Imagine …'	
2: 'By 9.20 …'	
3: 'You pause …'	
4: 'The lesson …'	
5: 'My response …'	
6: 'These communication …'	
7: 'The student …'	
8: 'Text message …'	
9: 'In the absence …'	
10: 'As for me …'	

b Why do you think the writer uses the
second-person form? How does it help to
make her article comic?

2 If the writer had written the article only in the
first-person form, how would it have sounded?

a Rewrite the first paragraph in the first
person, starting like this:

Imagine my first proper lesson …

b Comment on any problems you faced in
changing the paragraph to the first person.

3 a The writer uses some very short sentences:

The lesson is trashed.

I wince.

Find some more examples of simple sentences like these,
and describe the effect they have on the reader.

b Using simple sentences like these is one way in which the writer makes her style informal. Another is the vocabulary she chooses, for example, writing *trashed* instead of *ruined*. Take the following informal sentences and rewrite them in a more formal style. Choose more formal vocabulary and try using the third person, the past tense and a passive structure. The first example is done for you.

Informal	**Formal**
All you can hear are giggles …	*All that could be heard was laughter …*
Your punchy opening grabbed their interest.	
Get your students into the habit of switching off phones.	

4 The writer uses the present tense throughout her article. Instead, she might have written it in the first person using the past tense: *By 9.20 I was in full flow.*

Why do you think she uses the present tense? What effect does it have?

5 Persuasive texts sometimes use commands. Why does this writer use commands (look at the last-but-one paragraph)?

WRITING ACTIVITY

Some readers may feel that the writer gives a very one-sided view of mobile phones. Write a short response as a student, stating the case for mobile phones and why, used sensibly, they are valuable for students to have. Use a similar style to the writer's – that is, use the present tense and the second person. You might start like this:

Imagine you are a student. You are travelling to school. You realize you have left something vital at home …

Continue this text to make a strong case in favour of mobile phones. Develop your arguments in a way that is logical for the reader to follow.

Marketing
Improving Your Memory

Learning objectives

These texts are both aiming to market an idea. These are the objectives you will be studying:

- Word level: understand and explain what words mean in particular contexts

- Sentence level: explore the impact of a variety of sentence structures; look at different ways of grouping sentences into paragraphs; develop ways of linking paragraphs; adapt text types for different purposes; identify key changes when a text is changed from informal to formal

- Reading: follow themes and ideas; analyse the overall structure of a text

- Writing: present a case persuasively; develop and signpost arguments

---

Introduction

These two persuasive texts are about ways to improve your memory. The first is an advertisement that appeared in the *Independent* newspaper in 1997. The second is an American website which aims to persuade people that they could make better use of their memories.

The two texts use very different approaches. When you have studied them, you can write an advertisement of your own.

Glossary

feat – *achievement*

Text A

A Startling Memory Feat That You Can Do

How I learned the secret in one evening. It has helped me every day.

When my old friend Richard Faulkner invited me to a dinner party at his house, I little thought it would be the direct means of doubling my salary in less than two years.

Towards the end of the evening things began to drag a bit as they often do at parties. Finally someone suggested the old idea of having everyone do a 'party-piece'.

When it came to Peter Brown's turn, he said he had a simple 'trick' which he hoped we would like. First he asked to be blindfolded. Then he asked someone to shuffle a deck of cards and call them out in order. Still blindfolded he instantly named the cards in their order backwards and forwards without making a single mistake.

You may well imagine our amazement at Peter's remarkable memory feat.

On the way home that evening I asked Peter Brown how it was done. He said there was really nothing to it – simply a memory feat. Anyone could develop a good memory, he said, by following a few simple rules. And then he told me exactly how to do it.

What Peter said I took to heart. In one evening I made remarkable strides towards improving my memory. In just a few days I learned to do exactly what he had done.

The most gratifying thing about the improvement of my memory was the remarkable way it helped me in business and in my social life. I discovered that my memory training had literally put a razor edge on my mind. My thinking had become clearer, quicker, keener.

Then I noticed a marked improvement in my writing and conversational powers. What's more my salary has increased dramatically.

These are only a few of the hundreds of ways I have profited by my trained memory. No longer do I suffer the frustration of meeting people I know and not being able to recall their names. The moment I see someone I have met before a name leaps into my mind. Now I find it easy to recall everything I read. I can now master a subject in considerably less time than before. Price lists, reports, quotations, data of all kinds, I can recall in detail almost at will. I rarely make a mistake.

What Peter told me that eventful evening was this: 'Send for details of Dr Furst's Memory Course.' I did. That was my first step in learning to do all the remarkable things I have told you about. In fact, I was so impressed that I got permission to publish Dr Furst's Course myself.

My advice to you now is don't wait another minute. Full details of Dr Furst's remarkable Course are available free on request. Post the coupon today.

BOB HEAP

We, the publishers, have printed full details of Dr Furst's unique memory training method in a free book entitled 'Adventures in Memory'. For your free copy just post the coupon below (no stamp needed). Or write to: Memory and Concentration Studies, (Dept. IDM37), FREEPOST 246, London WC1A 1BR.

Text B

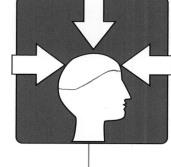

Do you realize how easy it is to improve your memory? Most people don't. In fact, most people do not realize the tremendous benefits an improved memory can have. They simply don't think about it; what they were born with is as good as it gets. Many people with poor memory usage may even think that they just aren't smart.

That's not true. **Anyone can improve their memory tremendously.**

If you noticed, we said 'poor memory usage' above and not 'poor memory'. That's because everyone has the potential to have an incredible memory. Most simply don't know the techniques that unleash this potential. By learning and using what we show you in our 'improved memory' document which will be available soon, you will be able to memorize lists of any number of items (10s, 100s, thousands); remember 10, 20, 50, 100+ digit numbers easily, learn how to never forget a person's name again, remember phone numbers, memorize entire decks of cards (suit and number) in order and out of order … Once you learn these techniques, the application possibilities are endless.

TRY THIS: Here's a quick example of a memory technique discussed in the document below:

Ever try to remember 10 things you needed to pick up at the grocery store and when you got there only remembered a few of the items? That will never happen again if you use this memory method! It uses numbers, rhymes and imagery to associate the desired items and commit them to memory, for as long as you want.

STEP ONE: Think of an image that rhymes with each individual number from 1 to 10. Once you decide on an image, be sure to use only that image from then on. Here is the list that we use:

1. NUN
2. SHOE
3. TREE
4. DOOR
5. HIVE (beehive)
6. STICKS
7. HEAVEN
8. GATE
9. WINE
10. HEN

Once you decide on your list, go through it a few times so that as soon as you say or think of a number, the image of the word you associated to that number comes to mind. You should be able to do this before going on to step 2.

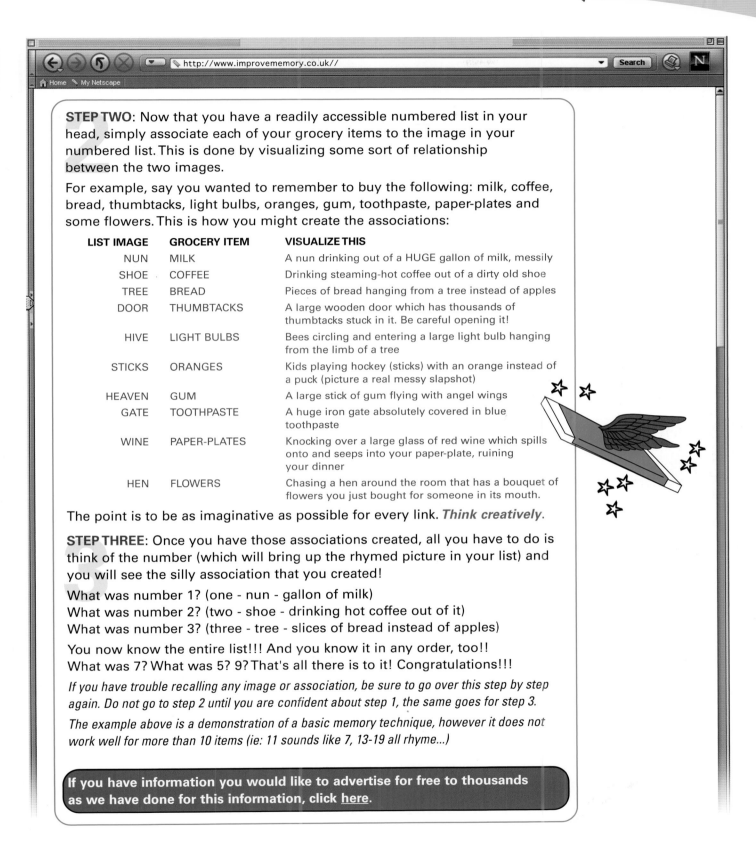

http://www.improvememory.co.uk//

STEP TWO: Now that you have a readily accessible numbered list in your head, simply associate each of your grocery items to the image in your numbered list. This is done by visualizing some sort of relationship between the two images.

For example, say you wanted to remember to buy the following: milk, coffee, bread, thumbtacks, light bulbs, oranges, gum, toothpaste, paper-plates and some flowers. This is how you might create the associations:

LIST IMAGE	GROCERY ITEM	VISUALIZE THIS
NUN	MILK	A nun drinking out of a HUGE gallon of milk, messily
SHOE	COFFEE	Drinking steaming-hot coffee out of a dirty old shoe
TREE	BREAD	Pieces of bread hanging from a tree instead of apples
DOOR	THUMBTACKS	A large wooden door which has thousands of thumbtacks stuck in it. Be careful opening it!
HIVE	LIGHT BULBS	Bees circling and entering a large light bulb hanging from the limb of a tree
STICKS	ORANGES	Kids playing hockey (sticks) with an orange instead of a puck (picture a real messy slapshot)
HEAVEN	GUM	A large stick of gum flying with angel wings
GATE	TOOTHPASTE	A huge iron gate absolutely covered in blue toothpaste
WINE	PAPER-PLATES	Knocking over a large glass of red wine which spills onto and seeps into your paper-plate, ruining your dinner
HEN	FLOWERS	Chasing a hen around the room that has a bouquet of flowers you just bought for someone in its mouth.

The point is to be as imaginative as possible for every link. ***Think creatively***.

STEP THREE: Once you have those associations created, all you have to do is think of the number (which will bring up the rhymed picture in your list) and you will see the silly association that you created!

What was number 1? (one - nun - gallon of milk)
What was number 2? (two - shoe - drinking hot coffee out of it)
What was number 3? (three - tree - slices of bread instead of apples)

You now know the entire list!!! And you know it in any order, too!!
What was 7? What was 5? 9? That's all there is to it! Congratulations!!!

If you have trouble recalling any image or association, be sure to go over this step by step again. Do not go to step 2 until you are confident about step 1, the same goes for step 3.

The example above is a demonstration of a basic memory technique, however it does not work well for more than 10 items (ie: 11 sounds like 7, 13-19 all rhyme...)

If you have information you would like to advertise for free to thousands as we have done for this information, click <u>here</u>.

3. 10 09

UNDERSTANDING THE TEXT

Text A

1 Who does the text seem to have been written by?

2 Who first made the writer aware of the possibility of improving his memory?

3 Name two ways that the memory improvements have helped the writer.

4 What do the publishers want readers to do next?

Text B

5 According to the text, who should be able to improve their memory?

6 Summarize the technique the writer uses to try to improve the reader's memory.

7 The technique described involves the reader in **visualizing** and in creating **associations**. Write down what you understand by these two terms as used here.

INTERPRETING THE TEXT

Text A

8 In small print at the top of the page it says *Advertisement*. Would you know without this heading that the text was an advertisement? Explain your answer.

9 a Why do you think the advertisement has been set out like a newspaper article?

b Do you think the advertisement would be more effective if it was presented in a different way (e.g. using more images, less text, a different approach)?

10 What would make readers want to send off for the free book 'Adventures in Memory'? What might they hope to gain?

Hints

- Think about what the book is supposed to do for the reader.

- Focus on the ways it will help them in different situations.

- Think about whether the reader has to pay for the book – what effect does this have?

Text B

11 This text aims to persuade us that we can improve our memory. Do you think it is trying to achieve anything else?

Hint

- Look at paragraph 3, beginning 'If you noticed', for a mention of something that will happen 'soon'.

12 Text A tries to persuade us by telling a story about Bob Heap. How does text B try to persuade us?

13 Text B is taken from a website. Which of these possible audiences do you think it is aimed at?

   a people with poor memories

   b people interested in the topic

   c a general audience

   d a young audience

   e people who want to succeed in business.

Choose the one or two descriptions that best fit. Then write a sentence or two explaining your choice.

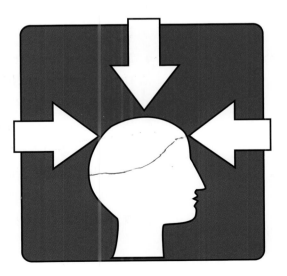

LANGUAGE AND STRUCTURE

Text A

1 Adverts are sometimes set out as newspaper stories. What features of layout make Text A look like a real newspaper article? Are there any features that do not?

2 Persuasive texts often use the first person (I) to express opinions, and the second person (you) for direct appeals to the reader. Find an example in the text of each of the following:

   a first-person statements about the writer

   b second-person commands addressed to the reader.

3 a Find a sentence that is designed to inform the reader.

   b Find a sentence that is designed to persuade the reader.

4 Text A uses a story structure, and some events are related in chronological order like a recount. Find three examples of connectives or linking phrases that the writer uses to link one idea with another *within* paragraphs, and three examples where he uses connectives *between* paragraphs.

Text B

5 This text does not use a first-person story. Instead, like many persuasive texts, it addresses the reader with hints and suggestions. Find an example of a sentence in the second person.

6 Persuasive texts try to link their ideas logically to help the reader follow them. Find three connectives used by this writer to join ideas together.

7 Persuasive texts often begin by stating what they are about, and then go through key points in detail.

   a What is the opening statement of this text (look at the first two paragraphs)?

   b Find three key points which follow this.

8 The writer uses a number of sentence functions to give the text variety.

    a Why do you think it begins with a question?

    b From the first paragraph, write down an example of a statement.

    c From anywhere in the text, write down an example of a command.

9 The writer addresses the reader directly using an informal tone. Find *three* examples of words or phrases that show the writer is aiming the text at the reader in an informal style.

WRITING ACTIVITY

10. 10. 09

Imagine that Bob Heap, the writer of text A, has discovered the memory technique described in text B. He writes about it for a newspaper advertisement. Write the first two paragraphs of the advertisement.

Remember to follow his style:

◆ retell it as a story

◆ use the first person (I)

◆ use the past tense.

You might start like this:

Improve your memory — it's as simple as 1-2-3!

One evening after a busy day in the office, I was relaxing by surfing the Internet. I'd always worried about my poor memory, so …

Extended writing

Imagine you have been asked to help promote a new interactive revision guide. RAPID REVISE is a CD-ROM for every Key Stage 3 and GCSE subject, which:

- lets students identify their own strengths and weaknesses
- uses video clips and a talking examiner to guide users through essential knowledge
- uses fun tests and instant feedback
- allows users to build their own revision schedule
- costs £12.

It is being marketed in two ways:

- An article to appear in magazines aimed at young people.
- A website giving users a flavour of what RAPID REVISE is like.

Write one or both of these persuasive texts.

For the magazine article:

- Think of your target audience – young people aged 13 to 16. How will you grab their attention? What main image might you use? How will you use layout?
- Think about the language style – will you tell a story, or address the reader directly?
- Will you write in the past or present tense?
- How will you persuade readers that they must buy the product?

For the website:

- How will you present the information?
- What interactive features might you use?
- How would you make the site eye-catching?
- Will you use an informal or formal style?
- Will you address the reader directly?
- How will you persuade readers that they must buy the product?

Advice texts: the essentials

Purpose and audience

- Advice texts aim to give us helpful information.

- Texts may aim to change our attitudes or behaviour, or encourage us to buy a product.

- They may be addressed to a particular audience – for example, a certain age group or gender – or to a specialist audience interested in their topic.

- Advice texts may share many of the features of instructions.

Text level features

- The text may use **illustrations** such as photographs and diagrams to help give clear advice.

- Often it will address the reader using the **second-person** form.

- To build the reader's confidence, it may use an **informal tone**.

Sentence level features

- To make the text more informal and more varied, the writer may use a **range of sentences**, especially simple and compound sentences.

- You would expect to find a range of **statements**, **questions** and **commands** in an advice text.

Word level features

- The writer will use some **description** where appropriate to make the advice easier to follow.

- Vocabulary will usually be **simple**, except where **technical terms** are necessary to discuss a specialist topic.

Health advice

A Sweet Tooth

Learning objectives

These texts offer different advice about eating sweets and your health. You will be studying the following objectives:

- Word level: work out the meaning of unfamiliar words; recognize how the formality of a text influences your choice of words

- Sentence level: look at a variety of sentence structures; explore changes in tense; adapt text types for different purposes; identify changes when a text is changed from informal to formal

- Reading: identify bias and objectivity; explore familiar themes by different writers

- Writing: reread work to anticipate a reader's reaction; present a case persuasively; give written advice which offers alternatives

Introduction

These three texts all give advice about sugary food. Text A is from a dentist's newsletter. Text B is an American website about chocolate. Text C is an opinion column from the *Star* newspaper. They give conflicting advice on what you should eat. When you have studied them, you can write your own advice text.

Text A

A change in your diet could improve your next check up

The main cause of tooth decay is SUGAR. Every time you eat or drink anything containing sugar your teeth are under attack for up to one hour.

The frequency of sugar consumption, more than quantity, is the important factor. It is best to limit sugary foods and drinks to meal times.

Many processed foods have sugar in them. Always read the ingredients labels when food shopping. Sugar can be called sucrose, fructose, glucose, lactose, dextrose and the higher up it appears in the ingredients list the more sugar is in the product.

To limit the frequency of consumption of sugar in your diet and help fight tooth decay:

- ✪ If you do eat sweet things, try to restrict them to meal times so the saliva produced can fight against the plaque acids.

- ✪ Try not to snack between meals. If you must, try raw vegetables, fruit, breadsticks, plain popcorn, low fat cheese or savoury sandwiches.

- ✪ Avoid sugary drinks between meals – drink water, milk, tea or coffee (without sugar: try one of the sweeteners if you can't do without).

- ✪ Also avoid strongly acidic drinks such as orange juice, all fizzy drinks (including diet and fizzy water) and sports drinks, which carry a risk of erosion of the enamel (dissolving the teeth). All these should be consumed in moderation. Never clean your teeth immediately after acidic drinks as it brushes the enamel away.

If you need further advice please ask the dentist or hygienist at your next appointment. Alternatively ask to see Becca who is studying to be a dental health educator - she will be able to identify causes of tooth decay in your diet and offer general advice on improving your oral health.

Text B

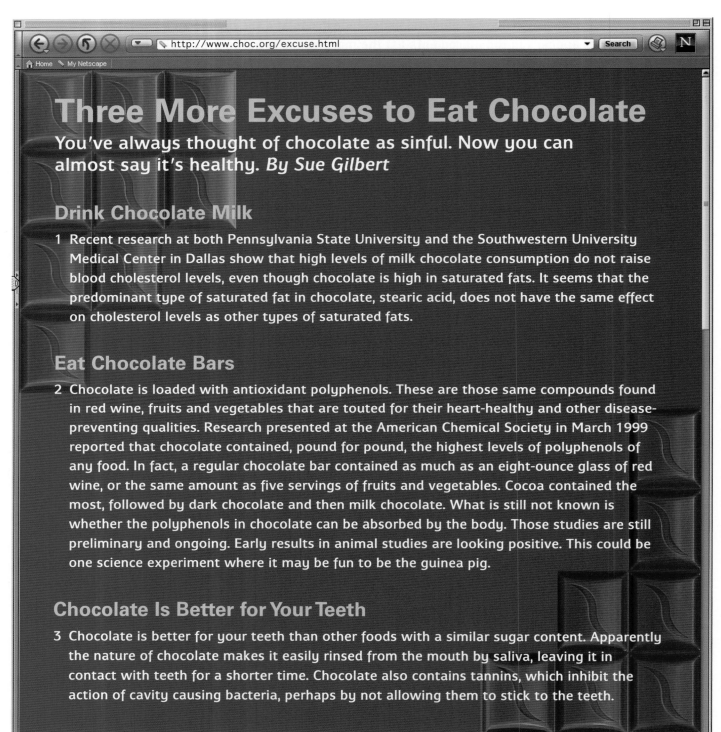

http://www.choc.org/excuse.html

Three More Excuses to Eat Chocolate

You've always thought of chocolate as sinful. Now you can almost say it's healthy. *By Sue Gilbert*

Drink Chocolate Milk

1 Recent research at both Pennsylvania State University and the Southwestern University Medical Center in Dallas show that high levels of milk chocolate consumption do not raise blood cholesterol levels, even though chocolate is high in saturated fats. It seems that the predominant type of saturated fat in chocolate, stearic acid, does not have the same effect on cholesterol levels as other types of saturated fats.

Eat Chocolate Bars

2 Chocolate is loaded with antioxidant polyphenols. These are those same compounds found in red wine, fruits and vegetables that are touted for their heart-healthy and other disease-preventing qualities. Research presented at the American Chemical Society in March 1999 reported that chocolate contained, pound for pound, the highest levels of polyphenols of any food. In fact, a regular chocolate bar contained as much as an eight-ounce glass of red wine, or the same amount as five servings of fruits and vegetables. Cocoa contained the most, followed by dark chocolate and then milk chocolate. What is still not known is whether the polyphenols in chocolate can be absorbed by the body. Those studies are still preliminary and ongoing. Early results in animal studies are looking positive. This could be one science experiment where it may be fun to be the guinea pig.

Chocolate Is Better for Your Teeth

3 Chocolate is better for your teeth than other foods with a similar sugar content. Apparently the nature of chocolate makes it easily rinsed from the mouth by saliva, leaving it in contact with teeth for a shorter time. Chocolate also contains tannins, which inhibit the action of cavity causing bacteria, perhaps by not allowing them to stick to the teeth.

Text C

OPINION
It's sweets and sour ...

SWEET-TOOTHED children are biting off more than they can chew – their teeth are rotting.

News from the British Dental Association that half of all five-year-olds and 90 per cent of 15-year-olds in the UK have tooth decay is alarming, but hardly surprising. Ask any parent who does not know the emotional blackmail which is created by a child bawling 'I want sweeties'.

Children become almost addicted to sugar with cravings for fizzy drinks and chocolate. Even if mum and dad are health conscious, the children still face peer pressure and resisting sweets displays at supermarket checkouts.

Dental health is important, which is why we owe it to our children to teach them about nutrition.

Stop before you buy them that next packet of sweets. After all, if you think they are crying hard at the refusal to give in, imagine the noise they'll make when they hear the dentist's drill ...

17.10.09.

UNDERSTANDING THE TEXT

Text A

1 How long do the damaging effects of sugar last?

2 Why should you try to eat sweet things only at meal times?

3 What should you do if you like the taste of sugar in tea or coffee?

Text B

4 Name two reasons the website gives that chocolate is 'almost' healthy.

5 Why is chocolate less damaging to your teeth than other sweets, according to the website?

Text C

6 What percentage of five-year-olds have tooth decay?

7 What two pieces of advice does the writer give to parents in the last two paragraphs?

INTERPRETING THE TEXT

8 All the texts are trying to advise the reader to do something. For each one write down what you think its purpose is, like this:

Text A is trying to advise us to ...
Text B is trying to advise us to ...
Text C is trying to advise us to ...

9 a Which text do you feel contains the most factual information, as opposed to opinion or theories? How can you tell?

b Which text seems most reliable and trustworthy? How can you tell?

10 Who do you think the three texts are aimed at? Use any of the descriptions below to help you define the target audience for each one:

mixed gender / single gender

young (below 16) / 16–35 / 35–60 / over 60 / no specific age group

educated readers / general audience / people with special interest in the subject/

people with something else in common

Give your response like this:

Text A seems to be aimed at ...	because ...
Text B seems to be aimed at ...	because ...
Text C seems to be aimed at ...	because ...

LANGUAGE AND STRUCTURE

1 Look at three headlines the texts use:

A: *A change in your diet could improve your next check up*

B: *Three more excuses to eat chocolate*

C: *It's sweets and sour*

The first headline addresses the reader directly.

The second offers a statement.

The third uses word play.

a Imagine Text A using a headline with word play. Here is a terrible pun it could use: 'The tooth, the whole tooth and nothing but the tooth'. Why would such a style not be appropriate for this text?

b Why do you think the writer of Text B uses the adjective *more* in the headline? Try to explain what she is hinting at.

c Headline C uses word play. This creates a slightly jokey tone. Why do you think the writer does this?

2 Although advice texts are generally written in simple language, they can use technical/scientific terms.

a Write down three words from each of Texts A and B which seem quite technical.

Text A		Text B	

b How can you work out the meanings of these words? Can you understand them from their form or context, or do you need to look in a dictionary?

C What do you think is the effect of using these technical terms? Choose the answer from below that you most agree with and complete the statement:

- ◆ it makes the text more difficult to follow because …
- ◆ it gives the text greater authority because …
- ◆ it teaches the reader something new because …
- ◆ it makes the writer seem more knowledgeable because …

3 Most advice texts use the second-person form to address the reader. Text A does this:

Every time **you** *eat or drink anything containing sugar your teeth are under attack for up to one hour.*

a Why do you think the writer has chosen to use the second-person form?

b How might the sentence be written in the third person?

c What is the effect when it is changed into the third person?

4 Look at Text B. Write down two connectives the writer uses to link one idea to the next.

5 Here are some of the language features of the three texts. For each one, try to find an example from the relevant text.

Sentence level features

Feature	Example
a Text A uses commands, with verbs at the start of sentences	
b Text B also uses commands occasionally	
c Text A uses the present tense	
d Text B uses the present tense	
e Text C mostly uses the present tense. Find an example of the future tense being used.	

Word level features

Feature	Example
f Text A uses adjectives and adverbs to add description	
g Text B uses formal rather than informal words. Write down a formal word and then an informal word that means the same thing. For example, Consumption (formal) ↔ eating (informal)	
h Write down some informal words used in Text C, and try to think of formal words that might be used instead for each.	

24. 10. 09.

WRITING ACTIVITY

Text B provides lots of information about why chocolate might be better for us than we thought. It is written in quite a technical style. Imagine you work for a chocolate manufacturer. How could you use the information to persuade people to start eating more chocolate? You might decide to produce a leaflet or poster encouraging customers to see the positive effects of eating chocolate.

Write one or two paragraphs for this poster or leaflet, using information from Text B. Address your advice to people who like chocolate, but feel guilty about eating too much of it.

Use:

◆ the second person (You …)

◆ facts

◆ an informal style

◆ the present tense.

When you have written your paragraphs, reread them and carefully consider the effect they will have on the reader. Do you need to change anything in your style or structure in order to make it more appealing to your audience?

Extended writing

Choose one of the topics below and write either a leaflet or a web page giving advice to the reader. Your advice should consist of:

a facts and statistics about the topic (you should research this)

b hints and advice on what to do.

Topics

Safe sunbathing:

* Why spending too much time in the sun is damaging
* How much time it is safe to spend in the sun
* Advice on ways of preventing burning

Exercise:

* Why exercise is important
* How much exercise people need
* Advice on different types of exercise

1 Choose your topic, then spend some time brainstorming ideas. To do this you could discuss the topic in a small group. If someone asked you for advice on the topic, what kind of response would you give?

2 Research the topic. It is important to give informed advice, which means providing factual information. You could use encyclopaedias; leaflets from supermarkets, gyms, or health centres; the library; the Internet.

3 Design your leaflet or website on one side of A4 paper. Make it visually interesting, but also clear and reassuring.

4 Think about how you will structure your advice: perhaps start with information, and then give your hints. Think about how you will use language. For example, will you:

* use the second person
* use a mix of statements, questions and commands
* use informal vocabulary which is easy to understand, rather than technical terms?

What are analytical texts?

Purpose and audience

Analytical texts give a response to other texts (e.g. books), to commercial products (e.g. a new type of car), or to media products (e.g. films). In schools, analytical texts are written by pupils to show their knowledge and understanding (e.g. history essays). Analytical writing often uses a broad question as its starting point – for example, 'What evidence is there that Lee Harvey Oswald did assassinate John F. Kennedy?'

Text level features

Analysis is often structured like this:

- opening statement
- exploration of the issue in general
- different key points discussed in turn
- a summary or conclusion.

When you are studying English, analysis of texts means exploring the themes, characters and language but not simply retelling the story. You will be expected to support points with evidence.

Sentence level features

The style is usually **impersonal**, using the **third person** for most of the analysis. The **first person** might be used for the conclusion. Texts are usually written in the **present tense**: 'Macbeth *is* desperate at this point in the play …'. **Connectives** will be used to help the reader compare and contrast ideas (*although, despite, similarly*) and to build arguments (*because, so, since, as a result*). They may also link to supporting evidence: *this shows that, we can see that.*

Word level features

Analytical texts will use relevant vocabulary for the subject under review (e.g. historical or scientific words, if appropriate). In English this will include **metalanguage** (language about language) such as *simile, rhythm, narrative*. There will also be vocabulary describing **judgements** (e.g. adjectives such as *entertaining, amusing*).

Analysing a process

How Rainforests Work

> ## Learning objectives
>
> This text analyses the issues surrounding rainforests. You will be studying the following objectives:
>
> - Word level: work out unfamiliar words; use a range of prepositions and connectives
>
> - Sentence level: explore changes in tense; understand the use of conditionals and modal verbs; develop ways of linking paragraphs
>
> - Reading: make notes in different ways; follow themes and ideas
>
> - Writing: present a case persuasively; develop and signpost arguments; present a balanced view; use evidence to support analysis and conclusions

Introduction

This text on rainforests is taken from an American website called 'How Things Work' (http://www.howstuffworks.com), which gives information on complex scientific issues.

Look at the way the writer presents information about the topic, giving different viewpoints before reaching his conclusion. When you have read his analysis, you can write one of your own.

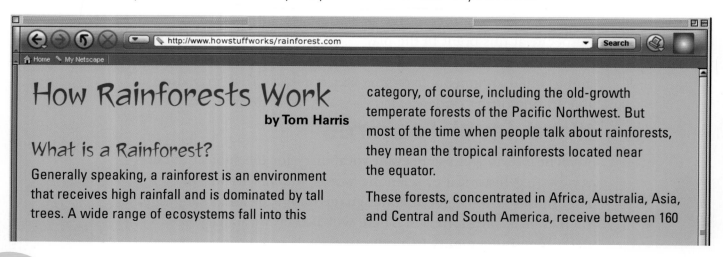

http://www.howstuffworks/rainforest.com   ▼ Search

🏠 Home ⚲ My Netscape

How Rainforests Work

by Tom Harris

What is a Rainforest?

Generally speaking, a rainforest is an environment that receives high rainfall and is dominated by tall trees. A wide range of ecosystems fall into this category, of course, including the old-growth temperate forests of the Pacific Northwest. But most of the time when people talk about rainforests, they mean the tropical rainforests located near the equator.

These forests, concentrated in Africa, Australia, Asia, and Central and South America, receive between 160

and 400 inches (406.4 to 1016 cm) of rain per year. Unlike the rainforests farther to the north and south, tropical rainforests don't really have a 'dry season'. In fact, they don't have distinct seasons at all. The total annual rainfall is spread pretty evenly throughout the year, and the temperature rarely dips below 60 degrees Fahrenheit (16 degrees Celsius).

Deforestation

In the past hundred years, humans have begun destroying rainforests at an alarming rate. Today, roughly 1.5 acres of rainforest are destroyed every second. People are cutting down the rainforests in pursuit of three major resources:

- ✿ Land for crops
- ✿ Lumber for paper and other wood products
- ✿ Land for livestock pastures

In the current economy, people obviously have a need for all of these resources. But almost all experts agree that, over time, we will suffer much more from the destruction of the rainforests than we will benefit. There are several factors involved in this scientific assessment:

- ✿ To begin with, the land in rainforest regions is not particularly suited for crops and livestock. Once the forest is cleared, it is even less so – without any decomposing plant life, the soil is so infertile that it is nearly useless for growing anything.

Generally, when people clear-cut a forest, they can only use the land for a year or two before the nutrients from the original plants are depleted, leaving a huge, barren tract of land.

- ✿ Cutting large sections of rainforest may be a good source of lumber right now, but in the long run it actually diminishes the world's lumber supply. Experts say that we should preserve most of the rainforests and harvest them only on a small scale. This way, we maintain a self-replenishing supply of lumber for the future.
- ✿ Rainforests are often called the world's pharmacy, because their diverse plant and animal populations make up a vast collection of potential medicines (not to mention food sources). More than 25 percent of the medicines we use today come from plants originating in rainforests, and these plants make up only a tiny fraction of the total collection of rainforest species.

The world's rainforests are an extremely valuable natural resource, to be sure, but not for their lumber or their land. They are the main cradle of life on Earth, and they hold millions of unique life forms that we have yet to discover. Destroying the rainforests is comparable to destroying an unknown planet - we have no idea what we're losing. If deforestation continues at its current rate, the world's tropical rainforests will be wiped out within 40 years.

UNDERSTANDING THE TEXT

1 Look again at the first paragraph. The writer says that the word 'rainforest' has a general meaning and a specific one.

  a What is the general meaning?

  b What are people more specifically thinking of when they mention 'rainforests'?

2 How rapidly are the rainforests being destroyed today?

3 One reason that humans destroy rainforests is to create 'livestock pastures'. What does this mean?

INTERPRETING THE TEXT

4 The writer gives a variety of reasons why preserving rainforests is important. Reread the text and make brief notes of the different reasons given.

LANGUAGE AND STRUCTURE

1 The writer uses two sub-headings: 'What is a rainforest?' and 'Deforestation'. What purpose do these serve?

2 Like most analytical texts, this one is mostly written in the present tense. However, in paragraph 3 the writer uses the past tense.

  a Which connecting phrase tells us that he is talking about the past?

  b Which verb phrase is written in the past tense?

  c Which connective does he use in the next sentence to show that the text is moving back into the present?

3 In the last sentence the writer uses the future tense, starting with a conditional clause, like this:

If deforestation continues …, rainforests will be wiped out.

Why do you think the writer finishes his analysis with a statement expressed in this way?

4 Look at the word *deforestation*. Even if you didn't know what the word meant, you could make a good guess by looking at different parts of the word.

    a Write down what you understand *deforestation* to mean.

    b Using a table like the one below, write down what each **morpheme** (part) of the word means:

Morpheme (part of a word)	What it means here
de-	
forest	
-ation	

WRITING ACTIVITY

The writer has strong opinions, and yet he writes without once using the pronoun I. He does sometimes use *we*. What if he were writing his analysis in a more personal form – perhaps a letter to the government? How would his style be different?

Using Tom Harris's article as your source, write the first two paragraphs of a letter analysing the consequences of destroying rainforests, and expressing your opinions. Write it as a letter addressed to the Head of Environmental Issues. You might start like this:

Dear Sir/Madam

I want to express my strong concerns at what is being done to the world's rainforests. It seems to me that the evidence shows …

Remember to:

- use the present tense
- use modal verbs to discuss possibilities: 'We *should* be working to …'
- use the first-person singular pronoun, *I*, to express your own feelings
- provide evidence, such as statistics, for what you say.

Giving facts and opinions
White Knuckle Rides

Learning objectives

These texts are guides or reviews, which give their readers factual information as well as opinions. These are the objectives you will study:

- Word level: recognize how the formality of a text influences your choice of words

- Sentence level: explore ways of grouping sentences into paragraphs

- Reading: identify bias and objectivity; explore how meaning changes when texts are adapted to different forms; recognize how texts are shaped by the technology they use; analyse the overall structure of a text

- Writing: organize information clearly; present a balanced view; use evidence to support analysis

Introduction

This unit features two texts. Text A is an extract from a newspaper review about British theme parks. It appeared in the *Independent*. Text B is from the *Independent* website. It is a guide to the 50 best white-knuckle rides in the world.

The two texts have very different styles. Both express views, supported by facts and statistics. Compare the way they present the facts and opinions. When you have studied these texts, you can write an analysis to review them.

Text A

Glossary

ascribed – *attributed*

contraption – *machine, invention*

cynical – *seeing the negative side of things*

The Complete Guide to British Theme Parks

Do you know your Hex from your Legend of Voodoo Mansion, Tidal Wave from Apocalypse? What's hot and what's not in Legoland and Gulliver's World? With so many sites to visit, it's hard to know where to start. Try here.
By **Martin Symington**

WHAT EXACTLY IS A THEME PARK ?

A beast that defies precise definition. Loosely, we are talking about a sizeable area devoted to fairground-type rides, rollercoasters, amusements and live shows. At some, there is a common 'theme' throughout, such as the 32m plastic bricks that lend Legoland in Windsor its distinctiveness, or the stories of Arthurian Legend and the Age of Chivalry that underlie Camelot Theme Park in Lancashire.

At other parks, specific themes are ascribed, seemingly randomly, to particular rides. Chessington World of Adventures' 'Rameses Revenge', for example, draws inspiration from the enigmas of ancient Egypt in order to clamp otherwise sane people into a contraption that turns them upside down, hurls them in various directions simultaneously, then dunks them in a pond (on the other hand, perhaps the ride's title is a reference to the effect the ride has on a participant's bowels).

Blackpool Leisure Beach has been a bit cleverer, theming rides according to the whims of corporate sponsors. Hence the 'Pepsi Max Big One' rollercoaster, and 'Playstation – the Ride', where you'll need to leave your game console

behind if you want to be catapulted vertically at 80mph before experiencing a freefall descent.

The cynical would suggest that there is one common theme to every park: money. Theme parks are in the business of separating punters from their cash, not just through entrance fees, but by selling fast food, soft drinks, trashy souvenirs and digital photos of families screaming on rollercoasters. And, where money's concerned, the more crowded the park the better.

AREN'T YOU JUST BEING AN OLD GRUMP ?

Not really. At weekends, school holidays and other peak times, most theme parks might as well be called 'Queue Gardens'. Dedicated theme-park goers and rollercoaster fans may think nothing of waiting for up to an hour for a five-minute ride (some even claim that anticipation enhances the experience, in the same way that the smell of cooking whets the appetite), but children who have been anticipating a fun day out for weeks see things rather differently; they hate queuing. The best way round this is to avoid weekends and holidays if you possibly can. Wet days are also quieter.

Text B

Glossary

fraught – *difficult, stressful*

`http://www.Independent.co.uk/travel/themes/activity/white knuckle` Search

Home My Netscape

50 Best ... White knuckle rides

'Woodies', 'airtime', 'inversions', 'G-roll': the language of coasters is as fraught as the business of riding them. So let **Emma Haughton** and her panel of experts experience the best rides going – so that you don't have to …

Pick and click for details

Best other thrills
Spiderman, Florida
Ice Blast, Blackpool
Vertigo, Wales
Tidal Wave, Surrey
Bounce, Wales
Dropzone, Ohio
Apocalypse, Staffordshire
The Giant Drop, Queensland

Best steel coaster
Nemesis, Staffordshire
Magnum XL-200, Ohio
Superman: Ride of Steel, Maryland
Millennium Force, Ohio
Incredible Hulk, Florida
Mindbender, Canada
Alpengeist, Virginia
Superman: The Escape, California
Steel Force, Pennsylvania
Montu, Florida

Medusa, New Jersey
Volcano, The Blast Coaster, Virginia
Dragon Khan, Spain
Raging Bull, Illinois
Big Thunder Mountain Railroad, France
Apollo's Chariot, Virginia
Texas Tornado, Texas
The Ultimate, North Yorkshire
Pepsimax Big One, Blackpool
Oblivion, Staffordshire
Kumba, Florida

Best wooden coaster
Tonerre De Zeus, France
Phoenix, Pennsylvania
The Beast, Ohio
Megafobia, Wales
Son of Beast, Ohio
Texas Giant, Texas
Coney Island Cyclone, New York
Stampida, Spain
Grand National, Blackpool
Comet, New York
Big Dipper, Blackpool
Raven, Indiana
Timber Wolf, Missouri
Wild Mouse, Blackpool
Thunderbolt, Pennsylvania
Cyclops, Wisconsin

Wild One, Maryland
Giant Dipper, California
Viper, Illinois
Riverside Cyclone, Massachusetts
Shivering Timbers, Michigan

The Panel
Steve O'Brien, 36, has been riding coasters since he was seven and is a regular contributor on **www.rollercoaster.com. Justin Garvanovic** is editor-in-chief of coaster magazine *First Drop* and founder of the European Coaster Club (**www.coasterclub.org**). **Andy Hine** is chairman and founder of the Roller Coaster Club of Great Britain (**www.rccgb.co.uk**). He has now sampled 90 per cent of the world's coasters. **Chris Cox**, 16, is a member of RCCGB and has experienced many of the world's best rides. He went on his first coaster at the age of six.

Best other thrills
Ice Blast, Blackpool
The UK's only 'vertical reality' air-powered experience, this £2m shot'n'drop tower stands at 210 feet, making it another major feature on the Blackpool skyline.
'More intense than Oakwood's The Bounce, this is a great way to be terrified and thrilled at the same time,' says Chris Cox. 'Definitely a must-have experience if you're ever in Blackpool.'

Where: Blackpool Pleasure Beach, Blackpool, Lancashire.
Ride duration: 1 minute.

Best other thrills
Dropzone, Ohio
Feel your heart plummet when you plunge 26 storeys from a height of 315 feet, straight down at speeds of over 61 mph. DropZone is the tallest gyro drop in the world – 'gyro' refers to the rotation on the way up, which gives you an outstanding view of the park and surrounding area. 'When it comes to freefalls, size does matter,' says Steve O'Brien. 'This offers the most gut-wrenching adrenalin-rush available.'

Where: Paramount's Kings Island, Kings Mills, Ohio, US.
Ride duration: 1 minute 28 seconds.

Best steel coaster
Nemesis, Staffordshire
Built in 1994, Nemesis opened as Europe's first suspended looping rollercoaster, and was voted the best steel coaster in Europe by the European Coaster Club last year. It cost £12m to build and runs for more than 2,350 feet, using 440 tons of steel. Riders are treated to an unnerving upside-down view of a blood-filled pool as they crest a 360-degree loop, which pulls four Gs on the way out. 'This is a classic,' says Justin Garvanovic, 'and it's so clever. The pacing is perfect and the terrain is used to excellent effect.'

Where: Alton Towers, Staffordshire.
Ride duration: 1 minute 30 seconds.

UNDERSTANDING THE TEXT

Text A

1 Based on the article, is it possible easily to sum up what a theme park is?

2 What is the main difference between the rides at Blackpool Leisure Beach and Chessington World of Adventures?

3 How should visitors avoid queues?

Text B

4 Where is the Nemesis ride?

5 How long does the Ice Blast ride last?

INTERPRETING THE TEXT

6 Do the two texts give the same information, or are they really covering the topics differently? Finish these statements:

  a Text A is about …

  b Text B is about …

  c The audience for Text A is probably …

  d The audience for Text B is probably …

  e What the texts have in common is that they …

  f They are different because they …

7 Analytical texts usually give both facts and opinions.

  a Find an example of a *fact* from Text A.

  b Find an example of an *opinion* from Text A.

  c Find an example of a *fact* from Text B.

  d Find an example of an *opinion* from Text B.

8 Text A is like a personal essay. Text B, for the most part, is much more factual. Which text do you prefer and why?

LANGUAGE AND STRUCTURE

1 Text A is organized in a question-and-answer format.

   a What do you notice about the style of the questions – how formal are they?

   b Why do you think the author has used this approach – how does it help him to communicate his message?

2 Text A uses some formal and complex words – such as *defies, devoted, distinctiveness*, which are all in the first paragraph.

   a Find three other complex words (words of more than two syllables, which are not familiar).

   b What does this choice of vocabulary tell you about the target audience?

3 Look at the way Text A is divided into paragraphs. For each paragraph, write down a few words to summarize what it is about.

4 The main page of Text B is much more direct, using hypertext links so that readers can choose what they wish to read next.

   a Why do you think the writer gives so little text on the main page?

   b Write a sentence or two describing the way the writer of the website pages has organized the material, and how this is different from the way it would be printed in a newspaper or magazine.

5 How would you describe the way the reviewers in Text B give their opinions?

   a their language is chatty

   b their language is informal

   c their language is quite formal

   d their language expresses their enthusiasm

   e their language gives an objective judgement.

Explain your choice.

6 Look at the box in Text B reviewing Nemesis. The review combines facts and opinions.

   a For each sentence, decide whether it is a fact (F) or an opinion (O):

      1: 'Built in …'

      2: 'It cost …'

      3: 'Riders are …'

      4: 'This is …'

      5: 'The pacing …'

   b Why do you think the writer has organized the mix of facts and opinions in this order?

   c How do the speech marks in the review make it easy to spot the opinion?

   d Why do you think the writer includes 'Where' and 'Ride duration' as a separate paragraph of information, rather than building it into the analysis?

WRITING ACTIVITY

How useful do you find the theme park and rollercoaster reviews? What are the best features of each text? What important information do they give? What do they tell you that is unnecessary? What questions do they not answer?

Write a paragraph or two answering these questions and analysing the two texts, saying which you prefer and why. Give quotations to support your arguments.

Unit 7

Extended writing

Choose one of the topics below and do some research on it:

- Students' opinions on the lunches served in your school canteen
- The television viewing patterns of people in your English class
- People's favourite type of chocolate bar.

This activity has four stages:

1 Plan your investigation

2 Do the research

3 Analyse the results

4 Write the analysis

You might work in pairs or small groups.

1 Choose your topic and plan your investigation. Decide exactly what you are aiming to find out. Set yourself a question – for example, 'What do students think of food served in school?'

Think about how you will get facts and opinions. You might use interviews, questionnaires, school data, and other sources.

2 Do the research. Make sure you are using a fair sample of people, but not too many. Make sure you are gaining facts ('How much television did you watch last night?') as well as opinions ('What type of programme do you like best?').

3 Analyse the results. Gather the responses together on a grid or chart. What patterns do you notice? What surprises are there?

4 Write the analysis. Start by explaining what question you intend to answer. Keep the style impersonal. Present the facts and opinions, perhaps using graphs, charts and diagrams. Write a conclusion based on the data. Build comments and quotations into your conclusion to support your points.

- Write in the present tense
- Avoid using the first-person singular (I)
- Use connectives to link ideas (*also, however, despite this* ...)
- Use layout features to make your report as clear as possible.

Speaking and listening
Special assignment

Learning objectives

This special assignment gives you the chance to analyse something through a discussion. These are the objectives you will be studying:

- Speaking: develop a spoken recount; ask questions to clarify meaning

- Listening: listen for a specific purpose

- Group discussion: think and talk about issues and ideas; take different roles in discussion

Discussing qualities

In pairs, discuss the qualities of something that both of you are familiar with. Possible topics might include:

- Which is the best theme park you have been to?

- Which is the best soap opera on TV — *Coronation Street*, *EastEnders* or another?

- Which is the best film you've ever seen?

- Which is the best novel you've ever read?

One of you should describe the product, place or event, giving examples of what makes it good. The aim is to try to think about why something is successful. Don't just say 'because I like it'!

For example, if you are discussing a soap opera, comment on how it's made, the topical issues it raises, the quality of the scripts and acting, the editing structure, how tension is created and so on. In other words, present some **evidence** to support your judgement.

Your listener should ask you questions in order to learn more about:

a the subject you are describing

b your own judgement of it.

When you have finished your discussion, swap roles to discuss a different topic.

What are reviews?

Purpose and audience

Reviews allow us to analyse, comment, and show the strengths and weaknesses of something. This might be a play, a book we have read, or a process, such as a project. Reviews will usually contain analysis (an account of what we notice), plus a judgement (what we think of it).

Text level features

The title may ask a **question**: 'How does Shakespeare create suspense in this scene?' The structure will usually be a **logical argument**, considering one point at a time, backing up each point with **evidence** (e.g. a quotation), and concluding with a personal **opinion** or summary of points.

Sentence level features

The style will often be **impersonal**, using the **third person** and avoiding saying I. It will usually be written in the **present tense**. Reviews use **connectives** to organize points, such as *although, however, therefore, this shows that.*

Word level features

The writer will use technical terms – for example, when discussing literature, words such as *plot, metaphor,* and *personification* will be used. The writer will include vocabulary related to **comment** – for example, *I thought … I expected … I learned that …,* when expressing a personal view.

UNIT 8

Writing about literature
Macbeth

Learning objectives

This extract is a critical essay on a set text. You will study the following objectives:

- Word level: use key terms to describe language; use the precise meaning of specialist vocabulary for each school subject; use a range of prepositions and connectives

- Sentence level: explore a variety of sentence structures; explore changes in tense; understand the use of conditionals and modal verbs; develop ways of linking paragraphs; know how to write in specific forms in particular subjects

- Reading: follow themes and ideas; analyse the overall structure of a text

- Writing: develop the use of commentary and description in narrative; give written advice which offers alternatives; use evidence to support analysis and conclusions

Introduction

In English you will often be asked to write about plays, poems and novels you have read. The idea is to demonstrate that you have understood the text, and can discuss your thoughts and ideas about it. A good essay will have an impersonal, slightly formal tone, rather than repeatedly using phrases such as *I think* … or *I like* …

The main part of an essay will explore different themes and ideas, supporting them with quotations from the text. The last section will aim to draw these ideas together. This section will probably be more personal.

This essay was written by Ben in Year 9. He was practising for his Key Stage 3 tests and the essay was written in timed conditions about Shakespeare's play *Macbeth*. When you have studied it, you can write a review of it.

Macbeth

In Act 4 Scene 1, Macbeth visits the witches to ask them to predict his future.

What do you learn about Macbeth's changing state of mind from the way he speaks and behaves in this scene?

You should think about:

- The way Macbeth speaks to the witches when he first appears;
- Macbeth's changing reactions to what the witches show him;
- What Macbeth's language tells you about his state of mind by the end of the scene.

From Macbeth's first reaction to the appearance of the witches, it is clear he doesn't like them. He seems to be horrified and yet fascinated by them. This is because witches were more real in Shakespeare's time than they are now. People today think of them as comic people with pointy hats and black cats. In the past they were much more threatening. Macbeth's fear shows this. He says:

> ' How now, you secret, black and midnight hags!
> What is't you do?'

He could have run away. Instead, he feels curious about who these 'weird sisters' might be. He also appears to be rude to them, addressing them as 'you secret, black and midnight hags'. This shows that he has no respect for them.

His attitude seems to change as they begin to make predictions. When they tell him to beware Macduff he becomes more interested. The witches may see that Macbeth looks shocked or nervous at this point because they say:

> 'Be bloody, bold, and resolute; laugh to scorn
> The power of man, for none of woman born
> Shall harm Macbeth.'

The witches are giving him advice on how to behave at this point. They seem to have a positive effect on Macbeth because he starts to believe that no one can harm him. He forgets their words of warning about Macduff. Macbeth didn't think this prophecy through properly, because he didn't think that Macduff could have been delivered through caesarean section.

The third apparition tells Macbeth:

'Be lion-mettled, proud, and take no care
Who chafes, who frets or where conspirers are.
Macbeth shall never vanquished be until
Great Birnam Wood to high Dunsinane Hill
Shall come against him.'

By this point, Macbeth seems to have become obsessed with himself and his future. He doesn't realise that an attacking army will cut down branches from Birnam Wood and use them to disguise their numbers. He has started to become arrogant, thinking that he is invincible.

When Macbeth finds out from the witches that Banquo's descendants will be kings, he becomes angry. He says:

'Horrible sight! Now I see 'tis true,
For the blood battered Banquo smiles upon me,
And points at them for his.'

Macbeth's language is full of fury. He uses alliteration 'blood battered Banquo' and this shows that he is aggressive, almost spitting out the words. By the end of the scene he is in a very angry state of mind. He has also become totally ruthless, shouting out orders to slaughter Macduff's family:

'The castle of Macduff I will surprise;
Seize upon Fife; give to th'edge o' th' sword
His wife, his babes and all unfortunate souls
That trace him in his line. No boasting like a fool;
This deed I'll do before this purpose cool.'

The scene shows Macbeth's changes of mood. He starts nervously, then becomes fascinated, then arrogant, and finally terrified. The witches leave him in a nervous state. After the show of eight kings Macbeth becomes extremely angry and takes out his anger on Macduff's family. It is not only his actions, but also his language which shows how power-crazed he has become. The actor playing Macbeth on stage would need to be able to show this range of feelings.

UNDERSTANDING THE TEXT

1 In his first paragraph Ben says that Macbeth feels two main reactions to the witches. What are they?

2 Why does Macbeth not run away from the witches, according to the essay?

3 What will happen with branches from Birnam Wood?

4 What point does Ben make about alliteration?

5 Write down a definition for a general reader of what alliteration means.

INTERPRETING THE TEXT

6 Good review writers should back up their arguments with evidence. How well do you think Ben supports his points? Does he use enough quotations? Are the quotations too long or too brief?

7 Literature students are often expected to say something about the context of a text – the period when it was written. Does Ben say anything about the play's context? Should he have said more, in your opinion?

8 When writing about plays, it is easy to treat them as if they are simply written texts rather than scripts to be performed. How well do you think Ben writes about the performance possibilities of the play?

9 What, overall, do you think the essay does well? How could Ben improve it? In your response you might refer to:

- structure
- use of quotations
- how he answers the question, and the way he develops his ideas
- knowledge of the text
- expression.

LANGUAGE AND STRUCTURE

1 Look at the first paragraph of Ben's essay. He uses sentences of different lengths:

From Macbeth's first reaction to the appearance of the witches, it is clear he doesn't like them.

Macbeth's fear shows this.

How does this variety of sentence length make his writing more interesting?

2 Essays are usually written in the present tense, as is most of Ben's.

a In the first paragraph he also uses the past tense. Find where he does this and explain why.

b In the last sentence of the essay, Ben uses a conditional verb:

*The actor playing Macbeth on stage **would need to ...***

Explain why he does this.

3 The ideas in a review need to be linked and structured using connectives. For each of the connectives below from Ben's essay, write down what its purpose is. The first is done for you:

Connective	Purpose
Instead (paragraph 2)	Shows something different – a contrast
This shows (paragraph 2)	
By this point (paragraph 6)	
The scene shows (paragraph 9)	

4 The concluding sections of reviews usually draw the arguments and ideas together, sometimes using personal comment, such as 'I think'. Does Ben's conclusion do this? Do you think what he writes is effective?

WRITING ACTIVITY

Imagine you are Ben's English teacher. You have just read his essay. What mark would you give it? What comments would you make?

Write a detailed commentary that will help Ben to see how well he has done and also give him some guidance on what to do next time. Use the second person (you) to address Ben directly.

Unit 8

Extended writing

Sometimes in English and other subjects you are asked to write essays. You will often be given a question to discuss, such as:

- *How does Henry V show his leadership skills in this scene?*
- *Some people think mobile telephones are an essential part of modern life. Other people see them as a menace. What are the arguments for and against them?*

This unit focuses on writing literature essays.

Your teacher will set you a specific title, based on a text you are studying. It might ask you to explore the way the main character changes, or how the writer builds tension in a particular scene.

Once you have your title, plan the structure of your essay:

1 Introduction describing the main issues or starting points (e.g. 'At the start of the scene, Henry is with his friends. He is part of the crowd, enjoying their jokes. He says: ...'

2 Main body of the essay, showing how ideas develop. Each point will be supported by a quotation or specific example. Connectives will help the reader to see how one idea links to another (e.g. '*This shows* Henry's different behaviour. He is *now* behaving in a more distant way. *Therefore it is clear* that ...')

3 Conclusion summarizing what you have learned (e.g. 'As the scene develops, Henry's character changes. At the start he was ...; by the end he is ...')

Write your first paragraph. Remember to:

- use a topic sentence that shows you are answering the question
- use an impersonal style (avoid *I* and *me* until the conclusion)
- use the present tense
- refer to the context of the text where possible (e.g. details about when it was written)
- use connectives and linking phrases to structure your argument (*at this point, later, it is clear, however*)
- use quotations to support your points
- use a variety of sentence lengths to keep your style interesting.

Assess Your Learning

Unit 5 Writing to persuade

Look back at the extended writing you did in response to the activity on page 72.

1 Complete a learning diary for it. Use the sentence starters below to help you.

What I did

To plan the content of the writing I ...

To organize my ideas I ...

To grab the reader's attention I ...

To make the layout interesting I ...

I addressed my readers directly because ...

To persuade my readers I ...

2 Give each aspect a star rating (* = least successful; ***** = most successful).

3 Think carefully about future targets and complete these sentences.

Targets

Next time, I will try to ...

To achieve this I will ...

Unit 6 Writing advice texts

With a partner, review the advice you wrote about safe sunbathing or exercise (p.82). Check whether you included the key features of advice texts shown in the spider diagram below.

Use informal vocabulary

Use presentation features to make the advice clear

Effective advice texts

Hook reader's interest

Use a mix of statements, questions and commands

1 Ask your partner to colour-code how successfully you used these features: green = very successful; yellow = partly successful; red = not successful.

2 Together, choose an aspect of your writing that you think is successful and explain why.

3 Choose an aspect of your writing that you think is less successful. Agree with your partner what you need to do to improve it.

Unit 7 Writing analysis

1 Work with the partner who you shared the speaking and listening assignment with, on page 96. Check that during the discussion you:

- used the present tense
- avoided using I
- used connectives to link your ideas
- used evidence to support your judgement
- gave facts as well as opinions.

Recall some specific examples, for example, some connectives you used, or a piece of factual evidence.

2 Discuss how you prepared for this speaking and listening activity. How useful was it? How might you prepare differently next time?

Unit 8 Writing reviews

In this unit you developed your knowledge about writing about literature. Read the following review of *Harry Potter and the Order of the Phoenix*.

> I have read all of the Harry Potter books and I really liked the fifth book though I sometimes felt that it went on a bit. The characters were the same as in the earlier books though there is no doubt that the central characters of Harry, Hermione and Ron have now grown up and are starting to see the world through more adult eyes.
>
> The plot was full of action, though at times I thought it moved a bit too slowly and in particular I thought the ending didn't really work because there were too many characters involved and it became quite confusing trying to follow exactly what had happened.
>
> The Order of the Phoenix is a nice idea – a group of wizards who are working against Voldemort's return, but I did think it was a bit long-winded at times.
>
> Overall I enjoyed the novel but felt it would have been better if it was a bit shorter.

Now comment on the review, identifying its strengths and weaknesses. Use the prompts below.

- Structure: How well are the ideas linked together?
- Vocabulary: How effectively does the writer use precise language?
- Evidence: How well does the writer provide evidence to support her comments?
- Tone: How well does the writer use an objective (detached) tone?

Write your comment on the review saying what works well and what could be done to improve it. Remember – the aim is to show your understanding of how to write effective reviews.

Getting started

Unit 9 Commentary and description

The best-selling writer John Connolly recently brought out a collection of ghost stories called *Nocturnes*. Read the opening of three of these stories.

a Steam and Fog swirled together upon the station platform, turning men and women to grey phantoms and creating traps for the unwary out of carelessly positioned cases and chests … ('The Underbury Witches')

b We should never have gone near Baaal's Pond. We should have stayed away from it as we were told, as we had always been told, but young men will follow young girls and do their bidding … ('Deep Dark Green')

c How should I begin this story? Once upon a time, perhaps; but, no, that's not right. That makes it a story of long ago and far away and it's not that kind of story. It's not that kind of story at all … ('The Erlking')

1 Working with a partner, decide which story opening:
- uses most description?
- gives hints about the character of the narrator?
- grabs your attention most?

2 Give each story opening a tension rating from low to high.

3 Choose one story opening and, with a partner, predict what you think happens next. Compare your predictions with others in your group.

Unit 10 Character and setting

1 Write the opening paragraph of a story. Use the hints below to create either a character or a setting. Make it as vivid and memorable as you can.

Character	Setting
• An elderly man	• A street on a Sunday morning
• Hunting for something	• Few people are around
• Moving through a park	• Music drifts from the window of a house
• Something is on his mind	• A dog is rummaging through a tipped-over dustbin

Spend four minutes working on your opening paragraph. Don't accept the first ideas that come into your head. Allow your mind to make connections, to see new thoughts, and to try out new ideas.

2 Compare your ideas with others in your group. Select the best ones and discuss why they are most effective.

Unit 11 Implying meaning

1 With a partner, choose a TV show and have a brief conversation about it (no more than one minute long). One of you should aim to be sarcastic about the programme. When you say 'it's a really entertaining programme' you really mean 'it's not a really interesting programme'. After the conversation, discuss how you conveyed the sarcasm and irony. Focus on the way:
- you moved your voice up and down (tone)
- you emphasized certain words
- you used eye-contact, facial expression and body language.

2 If you were writing the dialogue in a story, how would you show the reader that you were being sarcastic?

Unit 12 Imaginative treatments

Take the tale of *Goldilocks and the Three Bears* or *Little Red Riding Hood*. Working with a partner, think about how you could update the story to entertain the reader. For example, you could:
- make it into a *CrimeWatch* style programme in which a detective is investigating a crime
- tell it from a different character's point of view
- give the characters a different style of speaking (e.g slang)
- make it into a musical or opera.

Share your ideas with the class.

Unit 13 Forms of poetry

It's easy to believe that poetry isn't written or read much these days. In fact, we are surrounded by poetry. Working in a small group, brainstorm as many examples as you can of:

- lines from poems you have read at school (either recently or in the past)
- nursery rhymes
- lyrics from songs and raps
- words used in advertising jingles and slogans that are written like poems.

Addressing the reader directly

Introduction

When writers tell stories, they can choose to use any of a huge range of styles. These include either telling or showing. When a writer **tells** the reader something it might sound like this:

Many years ago there was an old, neglected castle ...

This approach will use description. Or the writer might address the reader directly, like this:

I want to tell you about an old, neglected castle ...

Showing usually involves getting readers to work out more details for themselves, like this:

The weeds around the castle had grown longer ...

This doesn't say directly that the castle is old or neglected, but hints at it by referring to weeds.

This unit looks at the way writers tell stories and, in particular, how they might address the reader directly to get us involved in the storyline.

The Umbrella Man

Learning objectives

You will be studying the following objectives:

- Sentence level: explore a variety of sentence structures
- Reading: analyse the overall structure of a text
- Writing: use commentary and description in narrative

The Umbrella Man

I'm going to tell you about a funny thing that happened to my mother and me yesterday evening. I am twelve years old and I'm a girl. My mother is thirty-four but I am nearly as tall as her already.

Yesterday afternoon, my mother took me up to London to see the dentist. He found one hole. It was in a back tooth and he filled it without hurting me too much. After that, we went to a café. I had a banana split and my mother had a cup of coffee. By the time we got up to leave, it was about six o'clock.

When we came out of the café it had started to rain. 'We must get a taxi,' my mother said. We were wearing ordinary hats and coats, and it was raining quite hard.

'Why don't we go back into the café and wait for it to stop?' I said. I wanted another of those banana splits. They were gorgeous.

'It isn't going to stop,' my mother said. 'We must get home.'

We stood on the pavement in the rain, looking for a taxi. Lots of them came by but they all had passengers inside them. 'I wish we had a car with a chauffeur,' my mother said.

Just then a man came up to us. He was a small man and he was pretty old, probably seventy or more. He raised his hat politely and said to my mother, 'Excuse me, I do hope you will excuse me …' He had a fine white moustache and bushy white eyebrows and a wrinkly pink face. He was sheltering under an umbrella which he held high over his head.

'Yes?' my mother said, very cool and distant.

'I wonder if I could ask a small favour of you,' he said. 'It is only a very small favour.'

I saw my mother looking at him suspiciously. She is a suspicious person, my mother. She is especially suspicious of two things – strange men and boiled eggs. When she cuts the top off a boiled egg, she pokes around inside it with her spoon as though expecting to find a mouse or something. With strange men, she has a golden rule which says, 'The nicer the man seems to be, the more suspicious you must become.' This little old man was particularly nice. He was polite. He was well-spoken. He was well-dressed. He was a real gentleman. The reason I knew he was a gentleman was because of his shoes. 'You can always spot a gentleman by the shoes he wears,' was another of my mother's favourite sayings. This man had beautiful brown shoes.

'The truth of the matter is,' the little man was saying, 'I've got myself into a bit of a scrape. I need some help. Not much I assure you. It's almost nothing, in fact, but I do need it. You see, madam, old people like me often become terribly forgetful …'

My mother's chin was up and she was staring down at him along the full length of her nose. It was a fearsome thing, this frosty-nosed stare of my mother's. Most people go to pieces completely when she gives it to them. I once saw my own headmistress begin to stammer and simper like an idiot when my mother gave her a really foul frosty-noser. But the little man on the pavement with the umbrella over his head didn't bat an eyelid. He gave a gentle smile and said, 'I beg you to believe me, madam, that I am not in the habit of stopping ladies in the street and telling them my troubles.'

'I should hope not,' my mother said.

I felt quite embarrassed by my mother's sharpness. I wanted to say to her, 'Oh, mummy, for heaven's sake, he's a very very old man, and he's sweet and polite, and he's in some sort of trouble, so don't be so beastly to him.' But I didn't say anything.

The little man shifted his umbrella from one hand to the other. 'I've never forgotten it before,' he said.

'You've never forgotten what?' my mother asked sternly.

'My wallet,' he said. 'I must have left it in my other jacket. Isn't that the silliest thing to do?'

'Are you asking me to give you money?' my mother said.

'Oh, good gracious me, no!' he cried. 'Heaven forbid I should ever do that!'

'Then what *are* you asking?' my mother said. 'Do hurry up. We're getting soaked to the skin here.'

'I know you are,' he said. 'And that is why I'm offering you this umbrella of mine to protect you, and to keep forever, if … if only …'

'If only what?' my mother said.

'If only you would give me in return a pound for my taxi-fare just to get me home.'

My mother was still suspicious. 'If you had no money in the first place,' she said, 'then how did you get here?'

'I walked,' he answered. 'Every day I go for a lovely long walk and then I summon a taxi to take me home. I do it every day of the year.'

'Why don't you walk home now?' my mother asked.

'Oh, I wish I could,' he said. 'I do wish I could. But I don't think I could manage it on these silly old legs of mine. I've gone too far already.'

My mother stood there chewing her lower lip. She was beginning to melt a bit, I could see that. And the idea of getting an umbrella to shelter under must have tempted her a good deal.

'It's a lovely umbrella,' the little man said.

'So I've noticed,' my mother said.

'It's silk,' he said.

'I can see that.'

'Then why don't you take it, madam,' he said. 'It cost me over twenty pounds, I promise you. But that's of no importance so long as I can get home and rest these old legs of mine.'

I saw my mother's hand feeling for the clasp of her purse. She saw me watching her. I was giving her one of my *own* frosty-nosed looks this time and she knew exactly what I was telling her. Now listen, mummy, I was telling her, you simply *musn't* take advantage of a tired old man in this way. It's a rotten thing to do. My mother paused and looked back at me. Then she said to the little man, 'I don't think it's quite right that I should take an umbrella from you worth twenty pounds. I think I'd better just *give* you the taxi-fare and be done with it.'

'No, no, no!' he cried. 'It's out of the question! I wouldn't dream of it! Not in a million years! I would never accept money from you like that! Take the umbrella, dear lady, and keep the rain off your shoulders!'

My mother gave me a triumphant sideways look. There you are, she was telling me. You're wrong. He *wants* me to have it.

She fished into her purse and took out a pound note. She held it out to the little man. He took it and handed her the umbrella. He pocketed the pound, raised his hat, gave a quick bow from the waist, and said, 'Thank you, madam, thank you.' Then he was gone.

'Come under here and keep dry, darling', my mother said. 'Aren't we lucky. I've never had a silk umbrella before, I couldn't afford it.'

'Why were you so horrid to him in the beginning?' I asked.

'I wanted to satisfy myself he wasn't a trickster,' she said. 'And I did. He was a gentleman. I'm very pleased I was able to help him.'

'Yes, mummy,' I said.

Roald Dahl

UNDERSTANDING THE TEXT

1 Look again at the first paragraph. Write down three facts we learn about the narrator of the story.

2 From the story as a whole, write down three things the narrator likes about the old man.

3 Why is the mother suspicious about the old man?

4 Why does she hesitate about whether to pay the old man for the umbrella?

INTERPRETING THE TEXT

5 Look at paragraph 9. The old man says: 'I wonder if I could ask a small favour of you …'. The writer then adds several paragraphs describing the mother's reaction before showing us what the favour is. What effect does he create by doing this?

6 Do you think the writer wants us to admire the mother, or to dislike her? How does he present her?

LANGUAGE AND STRUCTURE

1 Look more closely at the way the writer presents this story. He could have started it at the beginning of paragraph 2: 'Yesterday afternoon …'. Instead he begins with a direct address to the reader.

Why do you think he does this?

2 In the first paragraph the writer directly tells us information about the characters: 'I am twelve years old and I'm a girl …' Decide which of the reasons **a** to **d** you most agree with, and explain why:

a This approach makes the story more interesting.

b This approach makes the story seem more believable.

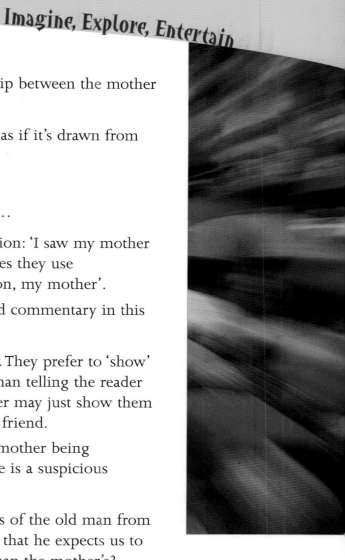

c This approach makes the relationship between the mother and daughter seem more realistic.

d This approach makes the story feel as if it's drawn from real life rather than made up.

Start your response:

The statement I most agree with is … because …

3 Sometimes fiction writers use description: 'I saw my mother looking at him suspiciously'. Sometimes they use commentary: 'She is a suspicious person, my mother'.

Find other examples of description and commentary in this text.

4 Some writers try to avoid commentary. They prefer to 'show' rather than 'tell'. For example, rather than telling the reader that a character is very mean, the writer may just show them not prepared to lend money to a close friend.

How could Roald Dahl have *shown* the mother being suspicious rather than by telling us 'she is a suspicious person'?

5 The writer presents two different views of the old man from the start of the story. How can you tell that he expects us to agree with the narrator's view rather than the mother's?

6 The writer uses a variety of sentence structures, including very short ones such as: 'They were gorgeous'. Find another example of a short, simple sentence in this text and describe its effect on the reader.

WRITING ACTIVITY

Rewrite the opening of the story so that you *show* the reader what the narrator is like without directly telling us that she is a girl aged 12, or that her mother is aged 34.

Then write a sentence or two explaining how easy or difficult it was to write your new opening paragraph, and how well you think it worked.

Unit 9

Extended writing

Take the story situation below. Write two versions of the story's opening sequence, using the two sets of style hints.

Story situation

X and Y (you can think up the names) have been friends since they were very young. Recently X has noticed that Y seems to be behaving differently. X wonders whether Y is unhappy, whether there are problems at home, whether she or he is under some other kind of pressure. X wants to discuss the situation but can't quite pluck up the courage. Then one night after school, X sees Y talking to two older men. They look suspicious. Y looks as if she or he is arguing with them. X sees Y walking away a few minutes later, and it seems as if Y has been crying.

Story styles

Story style 1	Story style 2
Tell the story in third-person style (using *she* or *he*)	Tell the story in the first person ('I')
Use the past tense	Tell it as though you are X
Show things rather than telling us (e.g. avoid saying 'Y was behaving strangely ...')	Address the reader directly: 'I am worried about ...'
	You might use a diary style
Decide at which point to start the story (e.g. in class earlier that day, in childhood when the two friends are playing, or with Y meeting the two men)	You might try using the present tense
	Use commentary as well as description: 'Y was behaving really strangely today ...'

Talk to a partner about the two story openings you have written. Which does he or she prefer and why?

Now write a one-paragraph commentary describing how well you think the two story openings work, and what you have learned.

In your commentary, focus on:

- the way you present the characters
- how much description you use
- the technique of commenting directly to the reader.

Figurative language

Writers often use language in imaginative, unexpected ways to present scenes and characters. This is called **figurative language**. You find it in all kinds of writing, including fiction, poetry and drama, as well as non-fiction text types such as advertising. This unit explores figurative language in fiction and poetry.

Figurative language might include the following:

Alliteration

This is the term used to describe a series of words next to or near each other, which all begin with the same consonant sound. This creates particular effects (e.g. **W**et, **w**indy **w**eather).

Emotive language

This is language that provokes a strong emotional response. Emotive words connected with fear might include: *dread, horror, terror*. Less emotive words might be *afraid, worried, scared*.

Hyperbole

This is exaggeration for the sake of emphasis or comic effect (e.g. *the journey took* **forever**).

Metaphor

Metaphor is the most common figure of speech. In metaphor, one thing is compared to another without using the linking words 'like' or 'as', so it is more direct than simile – one thing is actually said to be the other. For example, *My brother's room* **is a pig-sty**.

Onomatopoeia

This term refers to words that are thought to sound like the things they describe (e.g. *buzz, creak, murmur, bang, crash*).

Oxymoron

This is a figure of speech that combines two contrasting terms (e.g. *bitter sweet, living death, delicious hatred*).

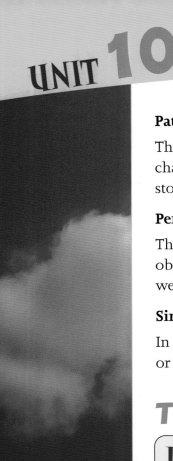

Pathetic fallacy

This means using natural settings to help describe the feelings of characters (e.g. a bright summer's day when someone is happy, a storm when terrified, rain when sad).

Personification

This is a form of figurative language in which animals, inanimate objects and abstract ideas are addressed or described as if they were human (e.g. *The sun refused to show its face*).

Simile

In a simile, two things are compared using the linking words 'like' or 'as'. For example, *My brother's room is **as** messy **as** a pig-sty.*

The Shipping News

Learning objectives

These are the objectives you will be studying:

- Word level: use key terms to describe language; appreciate figurative language
- Sentence level: explore a variety of sentence structures
- Reading: analyse the overall structure of a text
- Writing: experiment with figurative language for character and setting

Introduction

E. Annie Proulx writes novels set in bleak landscapes in North America. The following extract is taken from her novel *The Shipping News*. It is set in the remotest corner of Newfoundland, up against the Arctic Circle. In this scene, the hero Quoyle tries to rescue someone apparently drowned at sea.

Glossary

grapnel – *hooked grappling tool*

RCMP – *the Canadian national police force*

yawed – *turned from side to side*

broached – *took in water*

The Shipping News

There was no way down to the body unless he leaped into the foam. If he had brought a rope and grapnel … He began to climb back up the cliff. It struck him the man might have fallen from where he now climbed. Yet more likely from a boat. Tell someone.

Up on the headland again he ran. His sides aching. Tell someone about the dead man. When he reached the house it would take still another hour to drive around the bay to the RCMP station. Faster in the boat. The wind at his back swept his hair forward so that the ends snapped at his eyes. At first he felt the cold on his neck, but as he trotted over the rock he flushed with heat and had to unzip his jacket. A long time to get to the dock.

Caught in the urgency of it, that yellow corpse shuttling in and out, he cast free and set straight across the bay for Killick-Claw. As though there were still a chance to save the man. In ten minutes, as he moved out of the shelter of the lee shore and into the wind, he knew he'd made a mistake.

Had never had his boat in such rough water. The swells came at him broadside from the mouth of the bay, crests like cruel smiles. The boat rolled, rose up, dropped with sickening speed into the troughs. Instinctively he changed course, taking the waves at an angle on his bow. But now he was headed for a point northeast of Killick-Claw. Somewhere he would have to turn and make an east-southeast run for the harbour. In his experience Quoyle did not understand how to tack a zigzag across the bay, a long run with the wind and waves on his bow and then a short leg with the wind on his quarter. Halfway across he made a sudden turn toward Killick-Claw, presented his low, wide stern to the swell.

The boat wallowed about and a short length of line slid out from under the seat. It was knotted at one end, kinked and crimped at the other as if old knots had finally been untied. For the first time Quoyle got it – there was meaning in the knotted strings.

The boat pitched and plunged headlong, the bow digging into the loud water while the propeller raced. Quoyle was frightened. Each time, he lost the rudder and the boat yawed. In a few minutes his voyage ended. The bow struck like an axe, throwing the stern high. At once a wave seized, threw the boat broadside to the oncoming sea. It broached. Capsized. And Quoyle was flying under water.

In fifteen terrifying seconds he learned to swim well enough to reach the capsized boat and grasp the stilled propeller shaft. His weight pulled one side of the upturned stern down and lifted the bow a little, enough to catch an oncoming wave that twisted the boat, turned it over and filled it. Quoyle, tumbling through the transparent sea again, saw the pale boat below him, sinking, drifting casually down, the familiar details of its construction and paint becoming indistinct as it passed into the depths.

He came to the surface gasping, half blinded by some hot stuff in his eyes, and saw bloody water drip.

'Stupid,' he thought, 'stupid to drown with the children so small.' No life jackets, no floating oars, no sense. Up he rose on a swell, buoyed by body fat and a lungful of air. He was floating. A mile and a half from either shore Quoyle was floating in the cold waves. The piece of knotted twine drifted in front of him and about twenty feet away a red box bobbed – the plastic cooler for the ice he'd forgotten. He thrashed to the cooler through a flotilla of wooden matches that must have fallen into

the boat from the grocery bag. He remembered buying them. Guessed they would wash up on shore someday, tiny sticks with the heads washed away. Where would he be?

He gripped the handles of the cooler, rested his upper breast on the cover. Blood from his forehead or hairline but he didn't dare let go of the box to reach up and touch the wound. He could not remember being struck. The boat must have caught him as it went over.

The waves seemed montainous but he rose and fell with them like a chip, watched for the green curlers that shoved him under, the lifting sly crests that drove seawater into his nose.

The tide had been almost out when he saw the dead man, perhaps two hours ago. It must be on the turn now. His watch was gone.

E. Annie Proulx

UNDERSTANDING THE TEXT

1 Quoyle sees the person in the water but does not immediately try to rescue him. Why not?

2 Early on, Quoyle realizes he has made a mistake. What is it?

3 What are we told about Quoyle's ability to sail the boat?

4 In the water, what does Quoyle hold onto to stay afloat?

INTERPRETING THE TEXT

5 How does the writer show that Quoyle is anxious in the first two paragraphs?

6 The writer describes Quoyle, and shows us his thoughts ('"Stupid," he thought …'). What impression do you get of Quoyle from the extract?

LANGUAGE AND STRUCTURE

1 Look at these descriptions used by the writer, both of which contain similes:

The swells came at him broadside from the mouth of the bay, crests like cruel smiles.

The waves seemed mountainous but he rose and fell with them like a chip, watched for the green curlers that shoved him under, the lifting sly crests that drove seawater into his nose.

a Write down the phrases that contain similes.

b Notice how the writer describes the sea and waves. What technique does she use to make them seem threatening?

2 The writer sometimes uses very short sentences, and sometimes minor sentences (ones that do not contain a verb).

It struck him the man might have fallen from where he now climbed. **Yet more likely from a boat. Tell someone.**

Up on the headland again he ran. **His sides aching.**

[The boat] broached. Capsized. And Quoyle was flying under water.

a Rewrite these three examples using a more conventional (usual) style of punctuation.

b Say why you think the writer uses this style of very short sentences, and minor sentences. What effect does it have?

3 The writer structures the story to show how events lead to Quoyle being pitched into the rough sea. Look at paragraphs 1 to 6, and say what the topic is for each paragraph.

WRITING ACTIVITY

The writer describes events in a dramatic way. How would Quoyle himself later look back on what happened? Imagine that he is saved from the sea and recovers. Write the diary entry he might have written, describing how he came to be in the sea in the first place, and the thoughts and feelings he had. You could also make up how he might have been rescued, and describe that.

Unit 10 Extended writing

In the nineteenth century, engineers built a series of lighthouses around the coast of the British Isles. These were often built in places exposed to stormy seas, and involved dangerous journeys to isolated outcrops of rock.

Write a story or poem which uses figurative language to show these humans battling against nature.

Imagine a small team of people busy working on a small area of rock. The sky begins to darken and a terrible storm is clearly brewing. They can either try to escape by sailing their ship back to the mainland, or stay put and wait out the storm, sheltering in a tiny hut.

Use figurative language to capture the power of the storm and the desperate fear of the workers.

Write either in prose (as the opening of a story) or in verse (a poem).

The focus should be on the power of your language, rather than on the storyline itself. Try to give your language the power to show how terrible the storm really is. Use some of the language features mentioned in this unit: alliteration, emotive language, hyperbole, metaphor, onomatopoeia, oxymoron, personification, and simile.

Establishing tone

Naming of Parts

Learning objectives

You will be studying the following objectives:

- Word level: explore the meaning of words in quotation marks or used ironically

- Reading: identify bias and objectivity; explore implied and explicit meanings; analyse the overall structure of a text

- Writing: experiment with figurative language; explore how language can imply meaning and establish a specific tone

- Speaking and listening: recognize how messages are conveyed; explore ideas through role-play; work together to present and assess scripted and unscripted performances

Introduction

Writers can sometimes create powerful effects in their work by using language to hint at meanings rather than stating them directly. Think, for example, how sarcasm works in everyday conversation. You and a friend might be talking about someone else. One of you might say: 'That's a really fashionable haircut he's got'. Written on paper, the reader would assume that you meant what you said. But in speech, the tone of your voice might show that you mean the exact opposite – that it's not fashionable at all. In speech we show sarcasm through intonation, the way we move our voices up and down. In writing it's more complex.

This unit looks at the way a writer can create irony (the meaning beneath the surface being different from the meaning on the surface). It looks at the concept of tone – the way a writer's voice can help us to know her or his attitude to what is described.

Henry Reed's poem was written about the experience of being a soldier. It evokes the regular, repetitive drills and practices soldiers have to do – here, taking a rifle apart. Think about the tone of voice that should be used for reading the poem aloud.

Before reading

Work in pairs to read the poem aloud. Look at each stanza in two parts. One of you read the first four lines of each stanza as if you are a sergeant major on a parade ground. Then, from the beginning of the new sentence on the fourth line, your partner should read the rest in a gentler way. This will help you to explore the contrasting tones used in the poem.

Glossary

Japonica – *a plant with pink/red flowers*

Naming of Parts

Today we have naming of parts. Yesterday,
We had daily cleaning. And tomorrow morning,
We shall have what to do after firing. But today,
Today we have naming of parts. Japonica
Glistens like coral in all of the neighbouring gardens,
And today we have naming of parts.

This is the lower sling swivel. And this
Is the upper sling swivel, whose use you will see,
When you are given your slings. And this is the piling swivel,
Which in your case you have not got. The branches
Hold in the gardens their silent, eloquent gestures,
Which in our case we have not got.

This is the safety-catch, which is always released
With an easy flick of the thumb. And please do not let me
See anyone using his finger. You can do it quite easy
If you have any strength in your thumb. The blossoms
Are fragile and motionless, never letting anyone see
Any of them using their finger.

And this you can see is the bolt. The purpose of this
Is to open the breech, as you see. We can slide it
Rapidly backwards and forwards: we call this
Easing the spring. And rapidly backwards and forwards
The early bees are assaulting and fumbling the flowers:
They call it easing the Spring.

They call it easing the Spring: it is perfectly easy
If you have any strength in your thumb: like the bolt,
And the breech, and the cocking-piece, and the point of balance,
Which in our case we have not got; and the almond-blossom
Silent in all of the gardens and the bees going backwards and forwards,
For today we have naming of parts.

Henry Reed

UNDERSTANDING THE TEXT

1 Who do you think is the narrator of the first part of each stanza?

2 Who do you think the narrator is addressing?

3 The poet uses some technical words to do with rifles. Write down two examples.

4 He also uses specific names of flowers and plants. Write down two examples.

INTERPRETING THE TEXT

5 Look again at the first stanza. The writer uses the adverbs 'today', 'yesterday' and 'tomorrow'. Why do you think he refers to the present, past and future in this way?

6 What can we tell about the poet's attitude to the activity of naming the parts of rifles? Is he objective about it and merely presenting the scene, or does he have a message for the reader? Finish the sentence below that you think best sums up his response:

   a He thinks the activity is boring but necessary because …

   b He thinks the activity is pointless because …

   c He thinks the activity is very repetitive because …

   d He thinks the activity seems unnatural because …

   e He thinks the activity is mindless but better than being at war because …

7 What do you like or dislike about the poem?

LANGUAGE AND STRUCTURE

1 Look again at the first stanza. The writer uses the sentence 'Today we have naming of parts' three times. Why do you think he repeats it like this?

2 Each stanza has a similar structure: the first four lines describe the process of naming the parts of a rifle; the last lines describe nature.

   a What do you notice about words from the first part of each stanza that are repeated in the last part?

   b What tone of voice should be used for the first part of each verse?

   c What tone of voice should be used for the repeated words in the second part?

3 What do you notice about the vocabulary the writer uses in the different sections of each verse?

4 The poem is unusual becauses it uses 'we' and 'you', so that it sounds like a speech or discussion. How does this help the writer to show his attitude?

5 Put together a rehearsed reading of the poem. Work in pairs and practise getting the tone just right. Perform it as if it is a play.

WRITING ACTIVITY

Write a brief character description of whoever the poem is about. Who, for you, is the central character? Is it a sergeant major, or a raw recruit?

Imagine your character and write a paragraph about him based on your response to the poem. You might use similes or metaphors to make your description vivid.

Extended writing

Write a text called 'I love homework' (or something similar). Use it to experiment with tone of voice. You could write it as a poem, a monologue or dialogue.

On the surface, the text should seem as if it is genuinely saying 'I love homework'. The message to the reader should be, in fact, the opposite – that a lot of homework can be repetitive, boring, and exhausting.

Think about how you might create this contrast in meaning. How will you structure the writing?

You could write it in two parts: one spoken to a teacher, or by a teacher; the other, the thoughts of the pupil spoken inside her or his head.

Don't worry too much about rhythm and rhyme. The idea is to explore the tone of the text, to show an underlying meaning which differs from the surface meaning.

Here are some possible starting points:

A

I love homework
(*I'd only be watching TV, or out cycling, or learning something in the real world*)
I love all the writing
(*I'd only be writing to my friends or keeping in touch with a long-lost auntie*) . . .

B

I recommend homework
It's what makes me strong
Without all that practice
How would I know I was wrong? . . .

C

Tonight for homework you'll need to finish this poem
(*I thought poems were creative things*)
You'll need to write at least 15 lines
(*Whatever happened to free verse?*) . . .

Updating traditional tales

Arthur the King

Learning objectives

These are the objectives you will be studying:

- Word level: use key terms to describe language; appreciate figurative language

- Sentence level: explore a variety of sentence structures

- Reading: explore the conventions of common literary forms

- Writing: experiment with figurative language; explore unusual treatment of familiar material

Introduction

Some writers like to create their own characters and stories from scratch. Others work with existing tales. Shakespeare, for example, drew on stories from history and legend for almost all of his plays. Many other writers have done the same. Film-makers, also, often take material from the past and explore it for a modern audience. That is why we often have more than one version of a famous story (say, about the *Titanic*) – because each new generation retells the story in its own way.

Myths and legends lend themselves to this treatment. This unit looks at a version of the legend of King Arthur, one of England's earliest rulers. The author, Kevin Crossley-Holland, is famous for his reworking of legends. He retells this story through the eyes of Arthur himself, the boy who will one day become king.

Legends have their roots in a tradition of spoken stories, where people would pass on tales by word of mouth. Sometimes, therefore, even with modern writers, the storytelling style feels like spoken English.

Arthur the King

This falling snow is like an old man. It keeps forgetting itself, and wandering sideways. It doesn't really want to touch the ground. And now that the sun is shining, hazy, away in the west, the flakes look so frail you can almost see through them.

Sir Ector told me it was snowing when I was born. He said it was a fierce winter. Well, there have been many fierce winters since then: axe-winters, wolf-winters. There always will be.

Before my life ends, I want to describe my beginning – or, at least, the day that changed everything. I was twelve. So Kay, my elder brother, would have been six – no, seventeen. At any rate, I'm sure he had just been knighted, on All-Hallows' Day.

For several months after the death of King Uther – Uther Pendragon – the island of Britain had no king. True, Uther and Igraine, his queen, did have a son, but he had been entrusted to foster-parents when he was a baby, and only two people knew who they were: one was the old king himself, and he had gone to earth, like fallen snow; the other was the magician Merlin, and he wasn't telling.

When Uther died, everyone expected the foster-parents to claim the throne for their son, but this couple didn't realize they had the king's child in their care. So then the knights of the island began to talk and argue and lobby and squabble.

The Archbishop was worried. 'Our country needs a king,' he said, 'just as a king needs his fighting men and working men and praying men. We're like a ship without a rudder.'

Old Merlin agreed. He told the Archbishop to announce a tournament for New Year's Day, and then a great gathering at St Paul's, to choose the new king.

'Can I come?' I asked my father.

'You?' said Ector. 'I don't see why not.'

Kay wrinkled up his nose.

'Be fair, Kay!' said Ector. 'He's twelve. It's time he got the feel of things.'

On our way through London to our father's house, we saw quite a crowd of people in St Paul's churchyard. Sir Brastias was there! And Sir Tristram! And several dozen Londoners.

They had all gathered round a marvel: close to the east wall of the cathedral, there was a square plinth of shining green marble. A huge anvil had been set into the marble, and stuck into the anvil was a great gleaming sword.

Round the marble there were letters of gold. I read them for myself:

WHOEVER PULLS THIS SWORD

FROM THIS STONE AND ANVIL

IS THE TRUE-BORN KING

OF ALL BRITAIN

My father walked round the plinth. 'Where has this come from, then?' he said.

'Damned if I know!' said Brastias. He was copper-faced, and his nose was red.

'Well! What about it?' said my father.

'I can't move the damned thing,' said Brastias. 'How about you? How about it, King Ector?'

'How about King Kay?' said my brother.

Brastias looked at Kay and snorted. 'King Kay? King Kiss-curl, you mean! Never!'

First my father and then Kay stepped up on to the plinth and tried to pull the sword from the stone. But they couldn't do it. They couldn't move it a hair's breadth, and neither could any other knight who came to the churchyard.

I did wish I could try … But I wasn't a knight! I was only twelve.

Knights from moor and mountain, knights from marsh and fen: on New Year's morning, knights from all over the island armed themselves for the tournament.

I helped Kay put on his padded jacket and breastplate and thigh-plates and greaves and metal boots and, last of all, his helmet.

My father's servants, meanwhile, groomed and saddled our horses and tied Ector's and Kay's colours to their lances.

Just before we reached the tournament fields outside the city walls, Kay stood up in his saddle.

'My sword!' he exclaimed, clutching his sheath. 'It's gone!'

'Gone?' said Ector.

'I've left it behind,' wailed Kay. And then he rounded on me. 'You dressed me! Surely you noticed!'

'I … I …'

'It's not his fault,' said Ector.

'Go and get it!' said Kay. 'I need it. Please!'

I didn't want to turn my back on the distant shouts and braying trumpets, but I didn't want to let Kay down either. This was his first fighting tournament, and you can't fight without a sword. So I wheeled round and galloped back into London.

But when I got to my father's house, there was no one there – all the servants had gone to the tournament.

The door was locked; the windows were barred; I couldn't get in.

'What can I do?' I said. 'Kay must have a sword today.'

That was when I thought of the great gleaming blade: the sword in the stone.

I rode to the churchyard – there was nobody about; I tied my horse to the stile; I stepped up to the green marble plinth; I put my hand around the beautiful pommel, inlaid with precious stones.

Perhaps I was nervous, was I? Excited? What I remember now is such belief: a crowd of sparrows rushed across the churchyard, and I was confident and determined and joyous.

I scarcely had to pull the sword. It slid out of the anvil and flashed in the sunlight.

There was no time to waste! I galloped back to the tournament fields and gave the sword to my brother. He looked at it very carefully, then he looked at me, and his eyes brightened. I've seen that look of Kay's a hundred times. 'Father!' he called. 'Look at this!'

Ector came ambling over. 'You're back,' he said.

'Do you recognize it?' demanded Kay.

My father didn't say anything. He just stared at the sword.

'I'm the true-born king of all Britain,' crowed Kay.

'Where did you get that sword?' my father asked me.

'From the stone,' I replied. 'The house was locked and I couldn't get in, and Kay needs a sword for the tournament. It came out of the stone easily.'

'You?' said my father in a low voice. 'We're going back to the churchyard now.'

Kay and I weren't at all happy to be dragged away from the tournament, but there was nothing we could do about it. We had to turn our backs on all the excited hubbub, the brazen trumpets and the armed knights tilting and riding their challenges. We had to follow our father back into London.

Kevin Crossley-Holland

UNDERSTANDING THE TEXT

1 Look at the second paragraph. The narrator says '… it was snowing when I was born'. Who is the narrator of the story?

2 How old was the narrator on the day that his life changed?

3 What does the Archbishop mean when he says 'we're like a ship without a rudder'?

4 Why does Kay become angry with his brother?

5 How does the narrator feel when he tries pulling the sword from the stone?

INTERPRETING THE TEXT

6 Look at the opening sentence, a simile comparing the snow to an old man. What do you think the writer means by this?

7 Look more closely at the first section of the story. How does the writer make the reader want to read on?

8 Legends are usually set in a time long ago. How does this writer show that the story is set far in the past? Look for clues about:

 ◆ things that happen in the story

 ◆ the way people behave and are dressed

 ◆ the language used by the writer.

9 What impression do you get of the narrator in the story? Is he:

cocky   arrogant   innocent   foolhardy   pleasant   ambitious nervous?

Choose the word that best sums him up. Then write a sentence explaining your choice.

LANGUAGE AND STRUCTURE

1 Look again at the first sentence of the text. The writer uses the determiner 'this' rather than 'the'. What effect does this have?

2 At various points in the text the writer uses repetition of phrase structures, like this:

Well, there have been many fierce winters since then: **axe-winters, wolf-winters**.

So then the knights of the island began to **talk and argue and lobby and squabble**.

Knights from *moor and mountain,* **knights from** *marsh and fen …*

Use any of these examples and describe the effect of this repetition.

3 The writer uses some long, complex sentences, like this:

When Uther died, everyone expected the foster-parents to claim the throne for their son, but this couple didn't realize they had the king's child in their care.

He also uses short, simple sentences:

Old Merlin agreed.

Find a passage where a long and complex sentence is used near a short one, and describe the effects this has.

4 In some places the story feels as if it is being spoken to us rather than written down. Find an example, and explain what makes it seem like a spoken text.

Hints

Look at:

- the way the reader is addressed
- the types of details included
- how they are expressed.

WRITING ACTIVITY

The story is currently told using a first-person style. This means that the narrator tells us the story directly. Legends are usually told in a more impersonal style – for example, using the third person.

Take one short extract of the story and rewrite it using the third person. Make it feel more like a traditional legend.

You might begin like this:

Many years ago the snow fell thickly. It snowed like this when young Arthur was born and there had been many similarly bitter winters since then …

You can change the style as much as you wish.

Then write two or three sentences reflecting on the changes you have made, and the ways in which your version of the story feels different.

Unit 12 Extended writing

Write your own modern version of a story from the past. You might choose:

- a legend or tale from your local area

- a storyline from Shakespeare (e.g. *Macbeth*, retold in a modern way, perhaps as a thriller novel)

- an old poem retold as a piece of fiction (e.g. 'The Listeners' or 'The Highwayman').

Start by thinking about your audience. Who will you write your new version for? How old will the audience be? Will they already know the story, and, if so, what difference might this make?

Then start planning your writing. Think about how you will hook the reader's attention from the start. Will you address the reader directly, or use a more detached style?

- Will you use a dual narrative?

- Will you use third or first person?

- Will you update the setting of the story – for example, moving *Macbeth* from an old Scottish castle into a more modern location? Or will it chiefly be the language that you are updating?

Once you have completed your updated version, write a brief commentary reflecting on what you have done. For example:

- What changes have you made to the characters and storyline? How have you developed the language? How have you changed the setting?

- How pleased are you with the finished version? How well do you think it meets the needs of your target audience?

To get you started, here are three possible openings of an updated *Macbeth*. Working with a partner, discuss what you like and dislike about each one.

A Third-person description/traditional setting

The wind howled across the heath as night drew on. No one would have believed that, just hours before, this had been a place of bloodshed. A thousand men had lost their lives. Now it was dark and, except for the wind, silent ...

B First-person narration/traditional setting

If I look out from the top of the castle, the very top, I can see beyond the woods and across to a vast flat heath. I don't know which I hate more, the eerily creaking trees of the woods or the dreadful emptiness of the heath. I swore I'd never go there again. Now it looks as if I've got no choice.

C Commentary/modern setting

Where would you begin a story about evil? Not in a supermarket car park, I imagine. Not somewhere so ordinary, so undramatic. But that's where this story starts because that's where Macbeth's problems started. He was on leave, having some time off, and thought he would stock up the freezer. He drove into Tesco's as normal, past the filling station, up past the recycling centre, and something caught his eye. He assumed it was kids messing around. Shapes appearing and disappearing round the back of the bottle banks. Mind your own business, Macbeth. That's what he should have said. But that was his greatest mistake ...

Experimenting with styles

Introduction

Poetry comes in a huge range of styles and forms. Look down this list of just a few types of poetry:

Ballad – a narrative poem

Blank verse – verse that does not rhyme, usually written in iambic pentameter (10 beats per line)

Didactic – poetry that gives the reader advice or instruction

Dirge – a song to lament the death of a famous person

Dramatic monologue – a poem in which the speaker is not the author but a character

Eclogue – a conversation poem

Elegy – a poem to commemorate someone's death

Epic – a long narrative poem dealing with important matters

Epigram – a very short, witty poem

Epitaph – verse written on a tomb

Free verse – poetry that ignores traditional rhyme and rhythm structures

Haiku – a Japanese poem in three lines of five, seven and five syllables each

Idyll – a poem describing innocent people in ideal surroundings

Lament – a poem of mourning

Lampoon – a personal attack or caricature in verse

Lyric – a short poem expressing personal feelings

Mock heroic – a poem that describes trivial events in a very grand style

Narrative verse – a poem telling a story

Occasional verse – poetry written for a special occasion

Ode – a verse originally designed to be sung

Satire – a poem that ridicules the pomposity and vanity of humans

Sonnet – a poem of 14 lines with a particular rhyme scheme.

Love Poetry

This unit gives you the chance to compare the way two different poets approach the theme of love. One poem was written in the nineteenth century, the other in the twentieth century.

Both poems explore what it is like to have loved someone and then to feel alone.

Poem A

Sonnet

What lips my lips have kissed, and where, and why,
I have forgotten, and what arms have lain
Under my head till morning; but the rain
Is full of ghosts tonight, that tap and sigh
Upon the glass and listen for reply,
And in my heart there stirs a quiet pain
For unremembered lads that not again
Will turn to me at midnight with a cry.
Thus in the winter stands the lonely tree,
Nor knows what birds have vanished one by one,
Yet knows its boughs more silent than before:
I cannot say what loves have come and gone,
I only know that summer sang in me
A little while, that in me sings no more.

Edna St Vincent Millay

Poem B

Simple Lyric

When I think of her sparkling face
And of her body that rocked this way and that,
When I think of her laughter,
Her jubilance that filled me,
It's a wonder I'm not gone mad.

She is away and I cannot do what I want.
Other faces pale when I get close.
She is away and I cannot breathe her in.

The space her leaving has created
I have attempted to fill
With bodies that numbed upon touching,
Among them I expected her opposite,
And found only forgeries.

Her wholeness I know to be a fiction of my making,
Still I cannot dismiss the longing for her;
It is a craving for sensation new flesh
Cannot wholly calm or cancel,
It is perhaps for more than her.

At night above the parks the stars are swarming.
The streets are thick with nostalgia;
I move through senseless routine and insensitive chatter
As if her going did not matter.
She is away and I cannot breathe her in.
I am ill simply through wanting her.

Brian Patten

UNDERSTANDING THE TEXT

Poem A

1 Why is the narrator feeling sad?

2 What does she mean when she says 'the rain/Is full of ghosts tonight'?

3 What might she mean by 'unremembered lads'?

Poem B

4 Write down one detail the narrator remembers about the woman.

5 The narrator says: 'Her wholeness I know to be a fiction of my making'. What do you think he means by this?

6 At the end, what impression does the narrator give of his life now?

INTERPRETING THE TEXT

Poem A

7 The writer uses nature to show how the narrator feels. What do you think the following are supposed to symbolize?

   a Winter

   b Summer.

8 What picture do you get of the narrator – old, lonely, nostalgic, bored, unhappy? Use evidence from the poem to describe what she is like.

Poem B

9 The narrator is writing about someone who clearly means a lot to him. Why do you think the writer doesn't give her name?

10 What picture do you get of the narrator of this poem? How does he seem different from the narrator of Poem A?

11 What picture do you get from the two poems of the theme of love? Do they treat it differently, or do you gain a similar picture of what love feels like?

LANGUAGE AND STRUCTURE

1 Poem A has a more formal structure than Poem B. How can you tell?

2 Poem A is written as a sonnet, a 14-line poem with a particular rhyme pattern. Write down the rhyme scheme for the poem, using letters. To show which lines rhyme, use the same letter. The first part is done for you:

A B B A A …

3 Does Poem B use any rhyme?

4 Poet A structures her thoughts using connectives, such as: *And … Thus … Nor … Yet.*

   a How do these connectives give the poem a formal tone?

   b Poem B also uses connectives: *When … And … Still.* How do these make the poem seem less formal than Poem A?

5 Look at this statement:

Poem A uses formal vocabulary and lots of references to nature. Poem B is more personal and uses less formal vocabulary.

Do you agree? Write a short paragraph comparing the choice of vocabulary used in the two poems.

6 Look at the last line of Poem A, which finishes: '… that in me sings no more'. How might the writer have written this same idea if she were using a more colloquial (chatty) style?

WRITING ACTIVITY

Write a brief commentary on the two poems. Compare:

- the way they present the theme of love
- their use of metaphor
- the impression given of the two writers
- the similarities and differences in their styles.

Then say which you prefer and why. Remember to quote words and lines from the poems to support your arguments.

Unit 13 Extended writing

Choose a theme from the list below. Imagine there is to be a book of poetry on that theme. Write the opening parts of three poems, using a different style for each. Use the style checklist to help you.

Themes

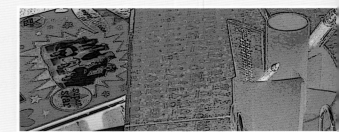

- Fear
- Falling out with a parent or friend
- Loneliness

Styles of poetry

Style checklist	Hints
Ballad – a narrative poem	Try to create a powerful rhythm. Tell the story at a rapid pace.
Didactic – a poem that gives the reader advice or instruction	Address the reader directly.
Epigram – a very short, witty poem	Aim for two or four lines.
Free verse – poetry that ignores traditional rhyme and rhythm structures	Structure your poem in any way you wish.
Haiku – a Japanese poem in three lines of five, seven and five syllables	Be strict in counting your syllables.
Lyric – a short poem expressing personal feelings	This should have a personal style, as if written about your own feelings.
Mock heroic – a poem that describes trivial events in a very grand style	Choose something insignificant like an argument over what to watch on TV, and present it as if it will lead to the world ending.

Remember that this activity is all about experimenting with poetry styles. A good starting point would be to spend some time looking though a poetry collection. This will help you to become familiar with the huge range of poetry styles that exist.

Once you have written your three fragments of poetry, you might show them as part of a class display, or talk to a small group about which style you found easiest and hardest to create.

Assess Your Learning

Unit 9 Commentary and description

Demonstrate your learning about the way writers tell stories using the two openings below. First, read them both carefully.

Story A	Story B
He sat in his lesson feeling uncomfortable. The whole class was being told off for misbehaving. The new teacher said she was unhappy about their conduct. He sat there feeling a sense of injustice. It wasn't him. He hadn't misbehaved at all. He had kept his head down and got on with his work. He started to put his hand up to tell the teacher, and then, just in time, changed his mind. It would only make matters worse. I sat there feeling miserable. Around me the chaotic noise had finally stopped. 'And another thing,' said Miss Crick, scanning the class over her glasses, catching each of our eyes in turn, 'you let me down personally with that kind of behaviour. Personally, you understand.'	A shadow fell across the playground as the sun slipped behind a heavy cloud. Even the sun was embarrassed. Should I say something, I wondered. Should I tell her that it wasn't me, that it wasn't fair? Out of my control, my hand snaked into the air, before I recaptured it and pulled it back.

1 Working with a partner, talk about: the use of description; the use of commentary (which reveals the thoughts and feelings of the narrator); the way things are shown rather than told; the way dialogue is used.

2 What do you like about each version? Which do you prefer overall, and why?

Unit 10 Character and setting

1 Look back at the piece of writing you did about the lighthouse builders of the nineteenth century (p.120). Copy and complete the grid below to reflect on the way you approached the task.

Language decision	Commentary
I chose to write poetry / prose because ...	
I approached the task by ...	
My first ideas included ...	
I used the following figurative devices ...	
The image I am most pleased with is ...	
Overall I think that the piece of writing is ...	

2 If you were starting the task again, how might you approach it differently?

Unit 11 Implying meaning

Think back to your joint presentation of the poem 'Naming of Parts' (p.124). Write a short paragraph explaining what you think was successful about it. Comment on: how you worked together to prepare your presentation; what your performance showed about your understanding of the poem; which presentation techniques (e.g. actions, tone of voice, pace) were successful; what you could have improved.

Share your comments with your partner. Do you agree with each other's judgements?

Unit 12 Imaginative treatments

1 In this unit you have explored the way writers sometimes update traditional tales. How is your understanding of writers' techniques developing? Chart your progress using the grid below.

Writer's technique	My understanding		
	Good	Reasonable	Poor
a) Using first- or third- person voice			
b) Using similes			
c) Using metaphors			
d) Using repetition of words and phrases			
e) Using a range of simple and complex sentences			

2 Now look at your own extended writing in which you retold a story from the past (p.133). Which of the techniques (a) to (e) did you use? Which technique do you think is most effective?

Unit 13 Forms of poetry

How has your understanding and writing of poetry developed? Complete a learning diary using the sentence starters below.

What I have read
Of the two poems I have read in this unit, I prefer _____ because ...

My views on poetry
There is more poetry around than people sometimes realize. For example ...
To capture emotions such as love, poets use techniques like _____. These help the reader by ...

What I have learned
In experimenting with different poetry styles, I learned ...
In writing a comparison of two poems, I learned how to ...
Aspects of poetry that I need to work on are ...

Getting started
Unit 14 Literary heritage

This unit explores the way texts relate to the time in which they were written. The first text was written in 1960; the second in 1838.

1 a Working in a small group, brainstorm anything you know about what life was like in the 1960s, for example, what sort of cars people drove, how they dressed, what domestic gadgets they used, what was happening historically. Draw pictures or make notes on one side of A4 paper to summarize your ideas.

b Now do the same for 1838. What do you know about the Victorian era? What was life like then? What technology existed? (Think of transport, factories, machines, etc.)

2 Look at the two historical photographs below. They both show scenes at school.

a What similarities and differences do you notice from the classroom you are currently in?

Look at:
- the way the pupils are dressed
- the way the teacher is dressed
- the room.

b What can you tell about attitudes to education and authority during these different times?

2 In the 1950s and 1960s, women and men were usually expected to have separate roles. In stories this often meant that boys would have all the active parts, while girls had supporting, more passive roles.

a Can you think of films, stories or television dramas where you have seen these stereotypes?

b Now think of an example of one that breaks the stereotypes by showing a woman taking a role that is as assertive and active as a man's.

4 Look at the image of Charles Dickens, author of *Nicholas Nickleby*. What impression do you get of him from the image? What can you tell about the period when he was writing from the way he is dressed?

5 Although you may not have read any books by Charles Dickens, you may know of his work from television and film adaptations, such as:

- *Oliver!*
- *A Christmas Carol*
- *Great Expectations.*

What do you already know about Charles Dickens's work?

6 One of the texts you are about to read is set in a school. It contains characters called Wackford Squeers, Mrs Squeers, Nicholas Nickleby and a boy called Smike. It is a boarding school where the boys are about to be given breakfast. Make some predictions about:

- what the characters will be like
- what the school will be like
- what will happen in the extract.

How texts reflect their culture

Introduction

Sometimes when we read literature, we forget about the time and place when the text was written. For example, it can be easy to ignore the world Shakespeare lived in, which was often brutal and disturbing. Also, knowing something about the theatre of his time can help us to understand the way he wrote. For example:

♦ plays were performed in inn yards around the country, and in open-air theatres in London

♦ performances took place by daylight

♦ there was little scenery – instead, the words of the play had to create the scene in the audience's mind

♦ plays would be aimed at all levels of society – so there needed to be something to appeal to everyone

♦ the stages brought the actors very close to the audience

♦ all the parts in a play were taken by men, never women.

The text we will study in this unit is much closer to our own times – it is by the twentieth-century children's author Enid Blyton. But it is still a reflection of its time.

Writing in the 1950s and 1960s, Enid Blyton had a huge influence on many children's early reading. After they had read her *Noddy* books, they would move on to the adventures of *The Secret Seven*, *The Famous Five*, and the *Mallory Towers* series.

With her strong emphasis on plot, Enid Blyton's adventure stories have entertained many thousands of readers. However, in reflecting the time when they were written, they show different values and attitudes – for example, in the way they present the roles of female and male characters. This extract is from one of the *Famous Five* books.

Five at Finniston Farm

Five at Finniston Farm

'Phew!' said Julian, mopping his wet forehead. 'What a day! Let's go and live at the Equator – it would be cool compared to this!'

He stood leaning on his bicycle, out of breath with a long steep ride up a hill. Dick grinned at him. 'You're out of training, Ju!' he said. 'Let's sit down for a bit and look at the view. We're pretty high up!'

They leaned their bicycles against a nearby gate and sat down, their backs against the lower bars. Below them spread the Dorset countryside, shimmering in the heat of the day, the distance almost lost in a blue haze. A small breeze came wandering round, and Julian sighed in relief.

'I'd never have come on this biking trip if I'd guessed it was going to be as hot as this!' he said. 'Good thing Anne didn't come – she'd have given up the first day.'

'George wouldn't have minded,' said Dick. 'She's game enough for anything.'

'Good old Georgina,' said Julian, shutting his eyes. 'I'll be glad to see the girls again. Fun to be on our own, of course – but things always seem to happen when the four of us are together.'

'*Five*, you mean,' said Dick, tipping his hat over his eyes.

'Don't forget old Timmy. What a dog! Never knew one that had such a wet lick as Tim. I say – won't it be fun to meet them all! Don't let's forget the time, Julian. Hey, wake up, ass! If we go to sleep now, we'll not be in time to meet the girls' bus.'

Julian was almost asleep. Dick looked at him and laughed. Then he looked at his watch, and did a little calculating. It was half past two.

'Let's see now – Anne and George will be on the bus that stops at Finniston Church at five past three,' he thought. 'Finniston is about a mile away, down this hill.

I'll give Julian fifteen minutes to have a nap – and hope to goodness I don't fall asleep myself!'

He felt his own eyes closing after a minute, and got up at once to walk about. The two girls and Tim *must* be met, because they would have suitcases with them, which the boys planned to wheel along on their bicycles.

The five were going to stay at a place called Finniston Farm, set on a hill above the little village of Finniston. None of them had been there before, nor even heard of it. It had all come about because George's mother had heard from an old school friend, who had told her that she was taking paying guests at her farm-house – and had asked her to recommend visitors to her. George had promptly said she would like to go there with her cousins in the summer holidays.

'Hope it's a decent place!' thought Dick, gazing down into the valley, where corn-fields waved in the little breeze. 'Anyway, we shall only be there for two weeks – and it *will* be fun to be together again.'

He looked at his watch. Time to go! He gave Julian a push. 'Hey – wake up!'

''Nother ten minutes,' muttered Julian, trying to turn over, as if he were in bed. He rolled against the gate-bars and fell on to the hard dry earth below. He sat up in surprise. 'Gosh – I thought I was in bed!' he said. 'My word, I could have gone on sleeping for hours.'

'Well, it's time to go and meet the bus,' said Dick. 'I've had to walk about all the time you were asleep, I was so afraid I'd go off myself. Come on, Julian – we really must go!'

They rode down the hill, going cautiously round the sharp corners, remembering how many times they had met herds of cows, wide farm-carts, tractors and the like, on their way through this great farming county. Ah – there was the village, at the bottom of the hill. It looked old and peaceful and half-asleep.

'Thank goodness it sells ginger-beer and ice-creams!'

said Dick, seeing a small shop with a big sign in the window. 'I feel as if I want to hang out my tongue, like Timmy does, I'm so thirsty!'

'Let's find the church and the bus-stop,' said Julian. 'I saw a spire as we rode down the hill, but it disappeared when we got near the bottom.'

'There's the bus!' said Dick, as he heard the noise of wheels rumbling along in the distance. 'Look, here it comes. We'll follow it.'

'There's Anne in it – and George, look!' shouted Julian. 'We're here exactly on time! Whoo-hoo, George!'

The bus came to a stop by the old church, and out jumped Anne and George, each with a suitcase – and out leapt old Timmy too, his tongue hanging down, very glad to be out of the hot, jerky, smelly bus.

'There are the boys!' shouted George, and waved wildly as the bus went off again. 'Julian! Dick! I'm so glad you're here to meet us!'

The two boys rode up, and jumped off their bikes, while Timmy leapt round them, barking madly. They thumped the girls on their backs, and grinned at them. 'Just the same old sixpences!' said Dick. 'You've got a spot on your chin, George, and why on *earth* have you tied your hair into a pony-tail, Anne?'

'You're not very polite, Dick,' said George, bumping him with her suitcase. 'I can't think why Anne and I looked forward so much to seeing you again. Here, take my suitcase – haven't you got any manners?'

'Plenty,' said Dick, and grabbed the case. 'I just can't get over Anne's new hair-do. I don't like it, Anne – do you Ju? Pony-tail! A donkey-tail would suit you better, Anne!'

'It's all right – it's just because the back of my neck was so hot,' said Anne, shaking her hair free in a hurry. She hated her brothers to find fault with her. Julian gave her arm a squeeze.

'Nice to see you both,' he said. 'What about some ginger-beer and ice-cream? There's a shop over there

that sells them. And I've a sudden longing for nice juicy plums!'

'You haven't said a *word* to Timmy yet,' said George, half-offended. 'He's been trotting round you and licking your hands – and he's so dreadfully hot and thirsty!'

'Shake paws, Tim,' said Dick, and Timmy politely put up his right paw. He shook hands with Julian too and then promptly went mad, careering about and almost knocking over a small boy on a bicycle.

'Come on, Tim – want an ice-cream?' said Dick, laying his hand on the big dog's head. 'Hark at him panting, George – I bet he wishes he could unzip his hairy coat and take it off! Don't you, Tim?'

'Woof!' said Tim, and slapped his tail against Dick's bare legs.

They all trooped into the ice-cream shop.

Enid Blyton

UNDERSTANDING THE TEXT

1 Where is the story set?

2 Write down the names of the members of the Famous Five.

3 Why are the children going to stay at Finniston Farm?

4 How can you tell that Dick is rude to his sister?

INTERPRETING THE TEXT

5 Write down three details from the story that show it is set in the past.

6 What do you notice about the way the characters talk which makes them sound different from the way most people speak today?

7 The text feels very sexist in places. Find an example of the way female and male characters are portrayed differently.

8 After Dick has teased Anne, 'Julian gave her arm a squeeze'. Why do you think he does this?

9 What can you tell about the different characters based on the extract? What are they like? Write down a sentence about each one.

10 What do you suppose will happen in the story? What has the writer done to prepare the reader for this?

LANGUAGE AND STRUCTURE

1 Look at the opening two paragraphs. They contain mostly dialogue. Notice how the writer uses exclamation marks at the end of many of the statements. Why do you think she uses these? What do they tell us about the way the characters speak?

2 Some of the dialogue feels old-fashioned, reflecting the time when the text was written. Look at this extract:

Don't let's forget the time, Julian. Hey, wake up, ass! If we go to sleep now, we'll not be in time to meet the girls' bus.

If you were writing the story today, how would you write this extract of dialogue?

a Write down your version.

b Write a sentence explaining what you have changed and why.

WRITING ACTIVITY

What would happen if you reversed some of the stereotypes in the story – for example, George teasing Dick about his haircut and the spot on his chin? Write a short version of the story in which:

- ◆ the girls are on their bikes waiting for the boys to arrive
- ◆ they meet them off a bus or train and tease them.

Use language in your descriptions and dialogue which shows the girls to be strong and independent, and the boys less confident. Compare different versions of the story written by people in your class.

Establishing the context
Nicholas Nickleby

Learning objectives

You will be studying the following objectives:

● Word level: appreciate figurative language; explore the meaning of words in quotation marks or used ironically

● Sentence level: combine clauses into complex sentences; make good use of punctuation; recognize key differences in texts from various historical periods

● Reading: use a range of reading strategies for independent research; explore implied and explicit meanings; identify links between texts and their context; recognize how texts relate to their culture

● Writing: experiment with figurative language; explore how language can imply meaning and establish tone

● Speaking and listening: reflect on your skills as a speaker; ask questions skilfully; recognize your skills as a listener; reflect on your skills in group discussions; use talk to question, hypothesize and speculate

Introduction

Charles Dickens's work is admired all over the world – he is perhaps the most famous novelist in English. He wrote at an amazing rate, publishing long novels in instalments which readers would eagerly await – a little like waiting for the next episode of a modern soap opera.

As well as creating an amazing gallery of memorable characters, Dickens also used his books to show the problems of the society of his day – for example, the poverty many people suffered, the terrible prison conditions and the dreadful education system.

In this extract from *Nicholas Nickleby*, he shows the terrors of a private school – Dootheboys Hall, run by Mr Wackford Squeers and his family. Here, on his first morning as a new school teacher, Nicholas sees the cruelty of the school, as Mrs Squeers fills the boys' stomachs with brimstone and treacle to spoil their appetites and stop them wanting to eat much breakfast.

Glossary

aversion – *dislike*

dogged – *constant*

malefactors – *criminals*

mercenary – *working only for money, grasping*

incipient – *early, just beginning*

brimstone – *sulphur*

corporal – *physical*

appropriation – *theft*

rueful – *sad*

physicking – *dosing with medicines*

distended – *filled out*

locomotion – *movement*

disconcerted – *concerned*

Nicholas Nickleby

'There,' said the schoolmaster as they stepped in together; 'this is our shop, Nickleby!'

It was such a crowded scene, and there were so many objects to attract attention, that, at first, Nicholas stared about him, really without seeing anything at all. By degrees, however, the place resolved itself into a bare and dirty room, with a couple of windows, whereof a tenth part might be of glass, the remainder being stopped up with old copy-books and paper. There were a couple of long old rickety desks, cut and notched, and inked, and damaged, in every possible way; two or three forms; a detached desk for Squeers; and another for his assistant. The ceiling was supported, like that of a barn, by cross-beams and rafters; and the walls were so stained and discoloured, that it was impossible to tell whether they had ever been touched with paint or whitewash.

But the pupils – the young noblemen! How the last faint traces of hope, the remotest glimmering of any good to be derived from his efforts in this den, faded from the mind of Nicholas as he looked in dismay around! Pale and haggard faces, lank and bony figures, children with the countenances of old men, deformities with irons upon their limbs, boys of stunted growth, and others whose long meagre legs would hardly bear their stooping bodies, all crowded on the view together; there were the bleared eye, the hare-lip, the crooked foot, and every ugliness or distortion that told of unnatural aversion conceived by parents for their offspring, or of young lives which, from the earliest dawn of infancy, had been one horrible endurance of cruelty and neglect. There were little faces which should have been handsome, darkened with the scowl of sullen, dogged suffering; there was childhood with the light of its eye quenched, its beauty gone, and its helplessness alone remaining; there were vicious-faced boys, brooding, with leaden eyes, like malefactors in a jail; and there were young creatures on whom the sins of their frail parents had descended, weeping even for the mercenary nurses they had known, and lonesome even in their loneliness. With every kindly sympathy and affection blasted in its birth, with every young and healthy feeling flogged and starved down, with every revengeful passion that can fester in swollen hearts, eating its evil way to their core in silence, what an incipient Hell was breeding here!

And yet this scene, painful as it was, had its grotesque features, which, in a less interested observer than Nicholas, might have provoked a smile. Mrs Squeers stood at one of the desks, presiding over an immense basin of brimstone and treacle, of which delicious compound she administered a large instalment to each boy in succession: using for the purpose a common wooden spoon, which might have been originally manufactured for some gigantic top, and which widened every young gentleman's mouth considerably: they being all obliged, under heavy corporal penalties, to take in the whole of the bowl at a gasp. In another corner, huddled together for companionship, were the little boys who had arrived on the preceding night, three of them in very large leather breeches, and two in old trousers, a something tighter fit than drawers are usually worn; at no great distance from these was seated the juvenile son and heir of Mr Squeers – a striking likeness of his father – kicking, with great vigour, under the hands of Smike, who was fitting upon him a pair of new boots that bore a most suspicious resemblance to those which the least of the little boys had worn on the journey down – as the little boy himself seemed to think, for he was regarding the appropriation with a look of most rueful amazement. Besides these, there was a long row of boys waiting, with countenances of no pleasant anticipation, to be treacled; and another file, who had just escaped from the infliction, making a variety of wry mouths indicative of anything but satisfaction. The whole were attired in such motley, ill-assorted, extraordinary garments, as would have been irresistibly ridiculous, but for the foul appearance of dirt, disorder, and disease, with which they were associated.

'Now,' said Squeers, giving the desk a great rap with his cane, which made half the little boys nearly jump out of their boots, 'is that physicking over?'

'Just over,' said Mrs Squeers, choking the last boy in her hurry, and tapping the crown of his head with the wooden spoon to restore him. 'Here, you Smike; take away now. Look sharp!'

Smike shuffled out with the basin, and Mrs Squeers having called up a little boy with a curly head, and wiped her hands upon it, hurried out after him into a species of wash-house, where there was a small fire and a large kettle, together with a number of little wooden bowls which were arranged upon a board.

Into these bowls, Mrs Squeers, assisted by the hungry servant, poured a brown composition, which looked like diluted pincushions without the covers, and was called porridge. A minute wedge of brown bread was inserted in each bowl, and when they had eaten their porridge by means of the bread, the boys ate the bread itself, and had finished their breakfast; whereupon Mr Squeers said, in a solemn voice, 'For what we have received, may the Lord make us truly thankful!' – and went away to his own.

Nicholas distended his stomach with a bowl of porridge, for much the same reason which induces some savages to swallow earth – lest they should be inconveniently hungry when there is nothing to eat. Having further disposed of a slice of bread and butter, allotted to him in virtue of his office, he sat himself down, to wait for school-time.

He could not but observe how silent and sad the boys all seemed to be. There was none of the noise and clamour of a schoolroom; none of its boisterous play, or hearty mirth. The children sat crouching and shivering together, and seemed to lack the spirit to move about. The only pupil who evinced the slightest tendency towards locomotion or playfulness was Master Squeers, and as his chief amusement was to tread upon the other boys' toes in his new boots, his flow of spirits was rather disagreeable than otherwise.

After some half-hour's delay, Mr Squeers reappeared, and the boys took their places and their books, of which latter commodity the average might be about one to eight learners. A few minutes having elapsed, during which Mr Squeers looked very profound, as if he had a perfect apprehension of what was inside all the books, and could say every word of their contents by heart if he only chose to take the trouble, that gentleman called up the first class.

Obedient to this summons there ranged themselves in front of the schoolmaster's desk, half-a-dozen scarecrows, out at knees and elbows, one of whom placed a torn and filthy book beneath his learned eye.

'This is the first class in English spelling and philosophy, Nickleby,' said Squeers, beckoning Nicholas to stand beside him. 'We'll get up a Latin one, and hand that over to you. Now, then, where's the first boy?'

'Please, sir, he's cleaning the back-parlour window,' said the temporary head of the philosophical class.

'So he is, to be sure,' rejoined Squeers. 'We go upon the practical mode of teaching, Nickleby; the regular education system. C-l-e-a-n, clean, verb active, to make bright, to scour. W-i-n, win, d-e-r, der, winder, a casement. When the boy knows this out of book, he goes and does it. It's just the same principle as the use of the globes. Where's the second boy?'

'Please, sir, he's weeding the garden,' replied a small voice.

'To be sure,' said Squeers, by no means disconcerted. 'So he is. B-o-t, bot, t-i-n, tin, bottin, n-e-y, ney, bottinney, noun substantive, a knowledge of plants. When he has learned that bottinney means a knowledge of plants, he goes and knows 'em. That's our system, Nickleby: what do you think of it?'

'It's very useful one, at any rate,' answered Nicholas.

Charles Dickens

UNDERSTANDING THE TEXT

1 How can you tell that the schoolroom is in a bad condition?

2 What is Nicholas's reaction to the sight of his new pupils?

3 How does Mrs Squeers give out the brimstone and treacle?

4 What does she then wipe her hands on?

5 Why is the sound of the classroom so different from what we would expect?

INTERPRETING THE TEXT

6 Why do you think the writer calls the hero by his first name – Nicholas – and the schoolmaster by his last name – Squeers?

7 What clues are there that the text is set in the past?

> # Hints
> - Look at things that happen in the story.
> - Look at the characters' use of language.

8 What can you tell about Nicholas's attitude to what he sees – is he disapproving or neutral?

9 How does Charles Dickens build our sympathy for the boys at the school, and make us dislike Squeers and his wife?

10 a What can you learn from the extract about the way private schools might have been organized and run in Dickens's time?

b Write a paragraph showing how the school described in the extract is different from the schools you have been in.

LANGUAGE AND STRUCTURE

1 To bring the scene to life, Charles Dickens uses some vivid descriptions, such as this one of the porridge:

a brown composition, which looked like diluted pincushions without the covers

What impression does this image create of the porridge?

2 One feature of Dickens's style is that he often uses very long, complex sentences. He also sometimes uses an elaborate or complicated way of expressing ideas. Look, for example, at this construction:

… the boys took their places and their books, of which latter commodity the average might be about one to eight learners.

How might you say this more simply?

3 Dickens's complex sentences often contain colons or semi-colons between the different phrases. Choose a sentence that includes at least one colon or semi-colon, and describe the job that the punctuation is doing in that sentence.

4 The text was written more than 150 years ago. What clues can you find in the language that hint at its age?

5 Paragraphs 2, 3 and 4 are very long – much longer than you would expect to see in most texts written today. Look at paragraph 4, beginning 'And yet this scene …'. If you had to divide it into shorter paragraphs, which of the sentences would you choose to start new paragraphs with?

6 As well as showing the terrible school conditions, Dickens also includes humour in the scene. He uses irony to hint at what is really going on, such as saying that young Squeers's new boots 'bore a most suspicious resemblance' to those previously seen on a new boy (paragraph 4). In the same paragraph, he uses a made-up word, 'treacled', to sum up what Mrs Squeers has done to the boys.

Choose a phrase or sentence that you find humorous, and explain its effects.

WRITING ACTIVITY

We don't see much of Nicholas's opinion of the school in the extract. Imagine the diary he might write that evening. He uses it to say how sickened he is by a) the school environment and b) the way the boys are treated by the Squeers family.

Write his diary entry for the evening that follows the events in the extract. Include vivid descriptions of the scenes he has witnessed.

Extended writing

Below is an extract from the stage version of the Nicholas Nickleby story. Written by playwright David Edgar, it is called *The Life and Adventures of Nicholas Nickleby*.

This extract shows how David Edgar uses a large cast to tell the story. The extract comes from the start of Part Two (which lasts in total about 4½ hours).

Glossary

tableau – *a silent group of people arranged to represent a scene*

sequestered – *sheltered, hidden from view*

bereaved – *having had a death in the family*

drudge – *person who does all the hard and unpleasant work*

The Life and Adventures of Nicholas Nickleby

Act One

Scene One

As the audience comes in, the Company mingles with them, welcoming them to the show. Eventually, the whole company assembles on stage. A Narrator steps forward, to start the re-cap of the story of Part One. During this Narration, the Company makes small tableaux that remind us of incidents in Part One.

Narrator: The story so far. There once lived, in a sequestered part of the county of Devonshire,

Mrs Nickleby: A mother,

Kate: And a daughter,

Nicholas: And a son.

Narrator: Who, recently bereaved, were forced to journey up to London, and to throw themselves upon the mercy of their only living relative, Ralph Nickleby.

Ralph: All three of 'em in London, damn 'em,

Noggs: He'd growled to his clerk,

Ralph: And you, sir? You're prepared to work?

Narrator: He'd demanded of his nephew, and receiving the firm answer

Nicholas: Yes!

Narrator: Ralph took young Nicholas and found him a position in a school in Yorkshire run by

Squeers: Mr Wackford Squeers.

Nicholas: Well, thank you, uncle. I will not forget this kindness.

Narrator: And arriving at the school, he met with

Mrs Squeers: Mrs Squeers,

Fanny: Their daughter Fanny,

Young Wackford: Their son young Wackford,

Narrator: And their poor drudge:

Mrs Squeers: Smike!

Narrator: And forty boys, with pale and haggard faces, lank and bony figures, children with the countenances of old men, all darkened with the scowl of sullen, dogged suffering.

Squeers: So – what d'you say?

Boys: For what we have received, may the Lord make us truly thankful.

David Edgar

Speaking and listening

1 Start by working in a group to think about how you would present this fast-paced storytelling sequence. How would it work on stage?

2 Discuss the way the writer compresses the storyline.

3 Discuss the way you get a glimpse of different characters.

4 Think about ways of making this sequence exciting to an audience who do not know anything about Charles Dickens.

Writing

1 Write about the ways in which the stage version feels different from the novel. You might comment on:

◆ the pace of the story

◆ the level of detail you get about characters and themes

◆ how far the writer has used similar language.

2 How do you think the text would work on stage? Write a description of the way you would present it if you were the director. How would you keep it moving quickly? How would you show the change of scenes?

Unit 14 Literary heritage

1 How confident are you at explaining the way texts reflect the time in which they were written? Use a traffic light system to show how your skills are developing.

⬤ I can do this well.

◯ I am doing quite well at this, but not all the time.

◯ I find this difficult to do.

Skill	Colour
I can spot details that suggest when a text was written.	◯
I can comment on the choice of words a writer makes.	◯
I can say something meaningful about the way a writer uses sentences.	◯
I can comment on how a text shows the attitudes that existed at the time (e.g. views about the role of women).	◯

2 Using the prompts below, reflect on what you have learned about life in 1960 and 1838 that you didn't know before.

What I have learned about ...	1960	1838
Roles of women and men		
Schools		
How life was different then from now		

3 a Make a list of the main differences in writing style between modern and older texts. Share your ideas with the class.

b With a partner, write a paragraph giving advice on what a modern reader should do to read older texts successfully.

Think about:

- two different ways they could work out the meaning of unfamiliar words. Find some examples to support your ideas.

- one reading strategy that you think is useful to help readers to follow the meaning of long sentences.

c With a partner, discuss what benefits you think there are of reading older literature. Try to think of three points. Compare your ideas with those from the rest of the class.

4 Look back at the speaking and listening task in which you reflected on the way *Nicholas Nickleby* was adapted for the stage. Think about your role in this process using the grid below.

Did you ...	How well?
● ask questions skilfully?	mostly – sometimes – not really
◆ listen well?	mostly – sometimes – not really
◆ take an active part in group discussions?	mostly – sometimes – not really
◆ use talk to question, hypothesize and speculate?	mostly – sometimes – not really

What two targets would you set yourself to improve your speaking and listening skills? Set one target for speaking skills and one for listening skills.

Targets:

-
-